access to history

in depth

PETER *the* GREAT

John Swift

Hodder & Stoughton

A MEMBER OF THE HODDER HEADLINE GROUP

Acknowledgements

The front cover illustration shows Peter I at Poltava by J.G. Dannhauer reproduced courtesy of Tretyakov Gallery, Moscow/The Bridgeman Art Library.

The publishers would like to thank the following individuals, institutions and companies for permission to reproduce copyright illustrations in this book:

Peter the Great by Falconet, Camera Press page 5; Princess Sophia by an unknown artist, Novosti (London) page 19; Augustus II, Dresden, Gemaeldagalerie, Alte Meister/AKG Photo, London page 35; Charles XII by David von Krafft, AKG Photo, London page 46; Peter the Great at the Battle of Poltava by G. Danhauer, Tretyakov Gallery, Moscow/The Bridgeman Art Library page 52; The Admiralty in St Petersburg by F. Alekseyev, Russian State Museum/SCALA page 67; Red Square in Moscow by F. Alekseyev, Tretyakov State Gallery/SCALA page 69; Catherine I by Jean Marc Nattier, St Petersburg, Hermitage Museum/SCALA page 99; The Mice Bury the Cat, AKG Photo, London page 112.

The publishers would also like to thank the following for permission to reproduce material in this book:

Macmillan Ltd for the extracts from *Peter the Great* by Vasili Klyuchevsky, Macmillan, 1963; The Orion Publishing Group Ltd for the extracts from *Peter the Great: His Life and World* by Robert K. Massie, Victor Gollancz, 1981; From *The Image of Peter the Great in Russian History and Thought* by Nicholas V. Riasanovsky. Copyright © 1992 by Oxford University Press, Inc. Used by permission of Oxford University Press, Inc. Thames & Hudson Ltd for the extract from *Peter the Great* by M.S. Anderson, Thames & Hudson, 1978; Yale University Press for the extract from *Russia in the Age of Peter the Great* by Lindsey Hughes, Yale University Press, 1998.

Every effort has been made to trace and acknowledge ownership of copyright. The publishers will be glad to make suitable arrangements with any copyright holders whom it has not been possible to contact.

Orders: please contact Bookpoint Ltd, 78 Milton Park, Abingdon, Oxon OX14 4TD. Telephone (44) 01235 827720, Fax: (44) 01235 400454. Lines are open from 9.00–6.00, Monday to Saturday, with a 24 hour message answering service. Email address: orders@bookpoint.co.uk

British Library Cataloguing in Publication Data
A catalogue record for this title is available from the British Library

ISBN 0 340 75814 7

First published 2000
Impression number 10 9 8 7 6 5 4 3 2 1
Year 2005 2004 2003 2002 2001 2000

Copyright © 2000 John Swift

Typeset by Fakenham Photosetting Limited, Fakenham, Norfolk
Printed in Great Britain for Hodder & Stoughton Educational, a division of Hodder Headline Plc, 338 Euston Road, London NW1 3BH by Redwood Books Ltd., Trowbridge, Wilts.

Contents

Preface

The original *Access to History* series was conceived as a collection of sets of books covering popular chronological periods in British history, together with the histories of other countries, such as France, Germany, Russia and the USA. This arrangement complemented the way in which history has traditionally been taught in sixth forms, colleges and universities. In recent years, however, other ways of dividing up the past have become increasingly popular. In particular, there has been a greater emphasis on studying relatively brief periods in considerable detail and on comparing similar historical phenomena in different countries. These developments have generated a demand for appropriate learning materials, and, in response, two new 'strands' have been added to the main series – *In Depth* and *Themes*. The new volumes build directly on the features that have made *Access to History* so popular.

To the general reader

Access books have been specifically designed to meet the needs of examination students, but they also have much to offer the general reader. The authors are committed to the belief that good history must not only be accurate, up-to-date and scholarly, but also clearly and attractively written. The main body of the text (excluding the Study Guide sections) should therefore form a readable and engaging survey of a topic. Moreover, each author has aimed not merely to provide as clear an explanation as possible of what happened in the past but also to stimulate readers and to challenge them into thinking for themselves about the past and its significance. Thus, although no prior knowledge is expected from the reader, he or she is treated as an intelligent and thinking person throughout. The author tends to share ideas and explore possibilities, instead of delivering so-called 'historical truths' from on high.

To the student reader

It is intended that *Access* books should be used by students studying history at a higher level. Its volumes are all designed to be working texts, which should be reasonably clear on a first reading but which will benefit from re-reading and close study.

To be an effective and successful student, you need to budget your time wisely. Hence you should think carefully about how important the material in a particular book is for you. If you simply need to acquire a general grasp of a topic, the following approach will probably be effective:

1. Read Chapter 1, which should give you an overview of the whole book, and think about its contents.

2. Skim through Chapter 2, paying particular attention to the 'Points to Consider' box and to the 'Key Issue' highlighted at the start of each section. Decide if you need to read the whole chapter.
3. If you do, read the chapter, stopping at the end of every sub-division of the text to make notes.
4. Repeat stage 2 (and stage 3 where appropriate) for the other chapters.

If, however, your course demands a detailed knowledge of the contents of the book, you will need to be correspondingly more thorough. There is no perfect way of studying, and it is particularly worthwhile experimenting with different styles of note-making to find the one that best suits you. Nevertheless the following plan of action is worth trying:

1. Read a whole chapter quickly, preferably at one sitting. Avoid the temptation – which may be very great – to make notes at this stage.
2. Study the diagram at the end of the chapter, ensuring that you understand the general 'shape' of what you have read.
3. Re-read the chapter more slowly, this time taking notes. You may well be amazed at how much more intelligible and straightforward the material seems on a second reading – and your notes will be correspondingly more useful to you when you have to write an essay or revise for an exam. In the long run, reading a chapter twice can, in fact, often save time. Be sure to make your notes in a clear, orderly fashion, and spread them out so that, if necessary, you can later add extra information.
4. The Study Guide will be particularly valuable for those taking AS level, A level and Higher. Read the advice on essay questions, and do tackle the specimen titles. (Remember that if learning is to be effective, it must be active. No one – alas – has yet devised any substitute for real effort. It is up to you to make up your own mind on the key issues in any topic.)
5. Attempt the source-based questions. The guidance on tackling these exercises is well worth reading and thinking about.

When you have finished the main chapters, go through the 'Further Reading' section. Remember that no single book can ever do more than introduce a topic, and it is to be hoped that, time permitting, you will want to read more widely. If *Access* books help you to discover just how diverse and fascinating the human past can be, the series will have succeeded in its aim – and you will experience that enthusiasm for the subject which, along with efficient learning, is the hallmark of the best students.

Robert Pearce

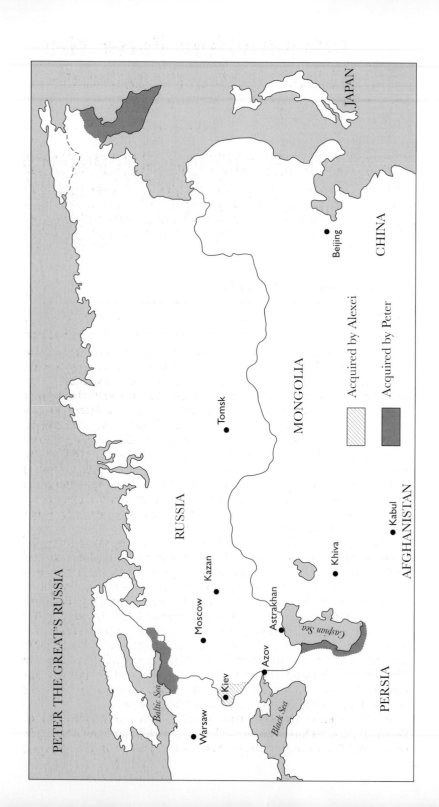

PETER THE GREAT'S RUSSIA

JAPAN

CHINA

• Beijing

Acquired by Alexei

Acquired by Peter

MONGOLIA

RUSSIA

• Tomsk

Kazan

• Moscow

Astrakhan

Caspian Sea

Khiva •

• Kabul

AFGHANISTAN

Warsaw •

Kiev •

Azov

Black Sea

Baltic Sea

PERSIA

1 Introduction: Peter the Great – the Historical Debate

POINTS TO CONSIDER

This chapter will introduce you to the various views of Peter the Great. Try to build a clear picture of why Peter may have deserved the title of 'the Great', and why his claims were subsequently challenged by historians.

1 The Claim to Greatness

KEY ISSUE What precisely was Peter's claim to greatness?

In October 1721, during the celebrations marking the end of the Great Northern War between Russia and Sweden, the Russian Senate urged tsar Peter to accept the titles 'Father of the Fatherland, Peter the Great, Emperor of All Russia'. It would be a mistake to assume that the Senate was acting spontaneously, or without Peter's knowledge. After some small show of modest hesitation – for the sake of form – Peter accepted. These were extravagant titles to claim. At the time, at least in Europe, the title of emperor was reserved to the Habsburg rulers of the Holy Roman Empire. Several states, including Britain, were sceptical of such pretensions and would not recognise the title for several years. Yet Peter, his supporters and subsequent admirers had no doubt that these titles were richly deserved. What then did Peter achieve to warrant such praise?

His reign (1682–1725) was, without doubt, a momentous one. His admirers argue that the Russia he inherited was weak, isolated and backward, but that by the end of his reign this had been changed drastically. In the field of foreign affairs Russia's standing had been transformed. In 1695 and 1696 he fought two campaigns against the Tatar Khanate of the Crimea (the powerful and feared vassal of the Ottoman empire), capturing Azov and bringing Russia near to a foothold on the shores of the Black Sea. Then between 1697 and 1698 he undertook his celebrated embassy to the west, visiting Prussia, the Netherlands, England, the Holy Roman Empire and Poland. He was thus the first tsar ever to travel abroad – at least the first not leading an invading army against his immediate neighbours.

In 1700 he entered the Great Northern War, as an ally of Poland and Denmark, against Sweden. This exhausting and bitter 21-year struggle dominated Peter's reign. It began badly with an abject and humiliating defeat for the Russians at the hands of a much smaller Swedish force at Narva (1700). As Charles XII of Sweden ignored Russia so that he could finish with Poland, tsar Peter organised the recovery of the Russian army. He gained a foothold on the Baltic Sea, regaining territory lost to the Swedes, which had been the aim of Russian tsars for generations. Here he founded his new capital, St. Petersburg (1703), and began the construction of a Russian Baltic fleet. When Charles XII finally turned to Russia, despite internal revolts, the Russians stunned Europe by inflicting a decisive defeat on the formidable Swedish army at Poltava (1709). Peter had difficulty exploiting his victory, however, as Charles XII refused to accept that his defeat was final. Peter soon found himself embroiled in a war with the Ottoman Empire and led his army to disaster on the river Pruth (1711). Only narrowly did he avoid a catastrophe as great as he had inflicted on the Swedes at Poltava. He lost Azov and might have lost everything he had won on the Baltic. The war with Sweden dragged on. It gave the Russians their first ever naval victory at Hangö (1714). But only well after Charles XII's death did the Russians secure the crucial Baltic territory they desired, through the Treaty of Nystadt (1721). This was not the end of Peter's wars. He led Russia into a further, less known war against Persia (1721–23), winning further territory by the Caspian Sea.

In all, Peter expanded Russia's frontiers, shattered the threat from Sweden and reduced Poland to a Russian client state. Even if the Turks remained a formidable threat, he had forced Russia out of its isolation and had made his nation a force to be reckoned with in international relations. Western Europe would never again be able to ignore Russia's interests – and even its existence – as the powers had previously done when they ordered the continent to their convenience. Yet Peter's claim to greatness is not based merely on his foreign policy successes. Underpinning his foreign policy there was a host of domestic reforms, the number and variety of which might suggest a fundamental reconstruction of Russia of even greater significance than all of Peter's foreign successes.

Simply to list Peter's internal reforms would be a pointless task. It should, however, be understood that there was no aspect of Russian life into which Peter would not intrude. To his admirers these intrusions were both necessary and beneficial. Whether it be the way Russians – the nobility if not the peasantry – dressed, which calendar and alphabet they used, how their children's marriages would be arranged or how they bequeathed their property, Peter issued a *ukaz* – a decree – and ordered a complete break with tradition, remaining indifferent to the sensibilities he had offended. He imported deeply detested foreign experts and foreign methods in his quest to modernise Russia's administration, military forces and economy. Yet it is argued that the offence he gave was necessary: Russia was not easily broken away from the confines of tradition, and the benefits of Peter's modernising reforms were immense.

These benefits can be summarised under a few broad headings. First, the transformation of the government. Peter abandoned the shambolic and medieval system of administration which he inherited, based as it was on a bewildering array of *prikazy* – government departments. This hotchpotch, with no clearly defined duties and often overlapping functions, was so inefficient that frequently even the tsar had no idea where to assign responsibilities. Peter replaced this muddle with a modern system of *kollegii* – colleges or ministries – under the supervision of a Senate. Not only the central administration, but local government was reformed, with a completely new structure of *gubernii* (governorships) and *uezdy* (districts), which was subsequently reformed into an even more elaborate system.

Second, in order to support his war effort he transformed the Russian economy. The construction of a modern army and the need to free Russia from dependence upon foreign suppliers encouraged Peter to set up domestic industries. The need for uniforms led to the establishment of textile factories. The need for guns led him to build up a metallurgy industry. The production of paper and sulphur, as well as shipbuilding and the construction of canals, were all fostered by Peter. He also saw the need for a class of Russian entrepreneurs and did his best to encourage their rise with loans and tariffs and the provision of labour. Despite false starts, failures and waste, it can be claimed that the foundations of Russia's industrialisation were laid by Peter.

Third, he was also responsible for the foundation of a modern education system, which broke with the tradition of Church controlled education and stressed technical skills. He sent Russians abroad to learn directly from the west. His reform of the alphabet and introduction of western-style books arguably founded a great literary tradition. He made education compulsory for the nobility. In short, he launched a major assault on the insular, xenophobic, hide-bound attitude of the nobility at least, thus effecting a fundamental change in their outlook.

Fourth, he also undertook a major Church reform, in which he firmly and irreversibly reduced the Russian Orthodox Church to the service of the state. Before Peter there were occasions when the patriarch (the head of the Russian Orthodox Church) was treated as the equal of the tsar. Peter abolished the office of patriarch, placing the Church under the authority of the Most Holy Synod – in reality an organ of the government. By reducing the Church to servility, it can be argued, Peter shattered traditional restraints on Russia's rulers and became in practice Russia's first *absolute* monarch – in theory ruling without any restraints on his power.

2 Supporters of the Claim to Greatness

> **KEY ISSUES** Who supported Peter's claim to greatness, and why?

In March 1725, Feofan Prokopovich, Archbishop of Novgorod and one of Peter the Great's closest collaborators, tearfully delivered the funeral oration to Peter. His eulogy was without restraint. He described Peter as the 'author of our innumerable blessings and joys, having as it were raised Russia from a state of death'. To Prokopovich, comparing Peter to the heroes of the Bible, he had been Russia's Samson for his victories; Japhet (a son of Noah) for his fleet; Moses for his laws; Solomon for his wisdom; and both David and the Roman Emperor Constantine for his Church reforms. Peter, he informed his equally tearful congregation:

> 1   hath left us, but ... the immense riches and fruits of his achievements, and glory are still with us; such as he has made Russia, such it will continue: he hath made it amiable to its friends; it will be belov'd by them: he hath made it terrible to its enemies; it will remain so: he hath made
> 5   it glorious throughout the whole World; it will never cease to be glorious: he hath left us directions and regulations, spiritual, civil, and military; therefore though his body is separated from us, his spirit remains with us ... And thou, O Russia! In considering what a prince thou hast lost, reflect how great he has left thee [sic].[1]

Prokopovich's eulogy summarised what became a basic part of the ideology of the Romanov dynasty. It was claimed that Peter had been personally responsible for the total transformation of Russia into a modern industrial state and a great power. From this view, Russian history could be divided into the pre-Petrine and post-Petrine periods. The former was medieval, superstitious, impoverished, weak and humiliated. The latter was modern, forward-looking, powerful and feared.

This view reached its peak with Catherine II (the Great) (reigned 1762–96). It was she who commissioned Falconet to cast the famous bronze statue of Peter which still stands in St Petersburg. This figure of Peter the Great, on horseback and pointing westward, remains one of the most enduring images of Russia's first emperor. On the base are the words 'Petro Primo, Catharina Secunda' – 'Peter I, Catherine II'. Catherine was attempting to strengthen her own entirely dubious claim to the Russian throne through association with the tsar reformer. She was reinforcing the legitimacy of her rule by presenting herself as the direct descendent of Peter in spirit, if not through any blood link. Furthermore by stressing the achievements of Peter, she also attempted to stress the even greater achievements she claimed for herself. Like other Russian rulers, she took it for granted that it was against the standard set by Peter that Russia

Statue of Peter the Great by Falconet.

measured the greatness of those who occupied its throne. To be seen as even greater than Peter was of immense importance to Catherine II. However well or poorly his successors might compare with him, there could be no doubt that Peter himself was a titanic figure in Russian history, and that his title of 'the Great' was richly deserved, if indeed it did not under-emphasise the magnitude of his achievements.

Though later historians questioned this view, it did occasionally become fashionable again. Under Stalin the image of Peter was used to complement Stalin's own 'cult of personality'; and now in post-Soviet Russia, with its political, social and economic uncertainties, there is a tendency to look for certainties and reassurance in the glories of the past. Thus the image of Peter the Great as a dominating individual in Russian history has again undergone a considerable revival. There are still modern western writers who tend to this view of Peter's greatness. Ian Grey, in *Peter the Great: Emperor of All Russia* (1960), concluded that his reforms, despite the frustrations and failures he experienced, 'affected every part of Russian life'. They were, indeed, 'the work of a careful legislator determined to introduce a new efficiency, wealth and well being into his country. To this end he issued a stream of *ukazi* which, gathering in a tidal wave, surged over Russia, transforming her irrecoverably'.[2]

3 The Search for an Objective View

> **KEY ISSUE** How was this claim to greatness challenged?

Initially it was rare indeed to find critics of Peter's greatness. Princess Catherine Dashkova, confidante of Catherine the Great, reflected the privately-held opinion of her empress when she said in private conversation that in her view Peter had been 'a cruel, crude, and ignorant tyrant' whose reforms had actually weakened the rule of law in Russia.[3] Such a view was noteworthy because it was so exceptional. The first writer of note who had the temerity to criticise Peter's reign publicly was Peter Chaadaev, in his first *Philosophical Letter* (1836). He dismissed Peter's attempts to bring civilisation to Russia as entirely ineffective. Scandalised, elite Russia rapidly concluded that Chaadaev was insane, and he had to make a hurried retraction. In *Apology of a Madman* (1837) he conformed to the standard view that Peter 'found in his hand a blank sheet of paper, and he wrote on it: Europe and the West'.[4]

A systematic examination of Peter's reign only became possible as the nineteenth century progressed and the Westerner and Slavophile controversy got under way. This was a passionate debate between sections of the Russian elite, concerning the future progress of the Russian state. The Westerners held – as their name suggests – that Russia had a common historic destiny with the west and must look to the west for the institutions, technology and political thought which would maintain its great power status. To the Westerners, Peter the Great remained a figure of inspiration. The Slavophiles disagreed entirely with this view. They denied a common historic destiny with the west. Russia, they held, must base its development on the values and institutions of its own early history. They believed that before Peter Russian society had been happy, peaceful and free of internal dissension, and that he had introduced the western class divisions, enmity and compulsion which had destroyed that society. Nicholas V. Raisanovsky summed up their case as being that Peter had:

> 1 introduced the principles of rationalism, legalism, and compulsion into
> Russia, where they proceeded to destroy or stunt the harmonious
> native development and to seduce the educated public. The Russian
> future lay clearly in a return to native principles, in overcoming the
> 5 western disease. After being cured, Russia would take its message of
> harmony and salvation to the discordant and dying West.[5]

In short, the Slavophiles believed that Peter's reign had been disastrous, as he had introduced foreign ideas and institutions which had corrupted an amicable society. Only by recovering that friendly society could Russia ever hope to fulfil its historical destiny and take up its rightful place as the moral, philosophical and political leader of the world. But no matter how disastrous they considered his reign, the Slavophiles never argued that Peter's rule had been anything less than titanic. He had transformed Russia for ill. They never argued that he had not changed Russia.

Only in the second half of the nineteenth century did more scholarly historical research appear, especially in the work of Sergei Soloviev (1820–79) and Vasily Klyuchevsky (1841–1911). This new generation of Russian historians sought to place Peter's reign in the context of the achievements of his predecessors. By emphasising the successes of Michael and Alexei, who ruled from 1613 to 1676, they downgraded the importance of Peter. They also stressed the failures, mistakes and often insignificant results of immense cost, effort and cruelty. Klyuchevsky, for example, saw Peter's reforms largely as the unsought results of his war effort. To him, Peter never really aimed for systematic reforms until the last decade of his reign, when victory was assured. Such views certainly reduced the role of Peter, but he remained a major historical figure.

This, in general, has been the conclusion reached by most modern historians. They tend to look at the terrible price Russia paid for Peter's reforms, especially in the degradation of the peasantry into a serfdom hardly distinguishable from chattel slavery – personal property, to be bought and sold at whim – whose only 'rights' were to be conscripted into the army or navy for life and to bear a crushing load in taxation. The evidence of their resentment in their rebellions and flight from authority is easily found. Paul Miliukov (1859–1943), among others, also looked closely at the effectiveness of Peter's reforms: at the number of commercial ventures he ordered set up which failed, at an immensely costly fleet and new capital that virtually no one wanted, at the education system which catered for only a few, and who were often hostile to it. They ask whether the changes were not more superficial than fundamental, and assess whether they were worth the price Russia paid for them. B.H. Sumner, in *Peter the Great and the Emergence of Russia* (1962), found that most of his reforms had precedents in hesitant steps made by his predecessors, but the unrelenting pace of change, the terrible burdens and cruelty which accompanied them gave the quite erroneous impression that Russia had broken fundamentally with the past. In reality, he took only a few steps which were completely without precedent: the abolition of the patriarchate, building a fleet, his new capital of St. Petersburg and sending Russians overseas. Robert K. Massie, *Peter the Great: his Life and World* (1981), laid greater stress on the inefficiency, corruption and resistance to change within Russia, and the huge cost of Peter's reforms, and concluded that his reign had a profound impact, but by no means as profound as has been suggested.

Other writers have taken such arguments further. To Lindsey Hughes, in *Russia in the age of Peter the Great* (1998), he enjoyed undoubted successes in foreign affairs, but won them by reinforcing servitude and autocracy, which left his successors with a tragic and ultimately ruinous legacy. M.S. Anderson, *Peter the Great* (1978), argued that Peter simply accelerated and intensified greatly changes already in progress: an evolution which again only seemed revolutionary. The passive resistance of the Russian people did much to frustrate his reforms, many of which could not be effectively enforced. Indeed, Anderson concluded, much of his legislation 'was mere futile nagging, which was soon forgotten and had no practical effect'.[6] Alex de Jonge, *Fire and Water: a Life of Peter the Great* (1979), suggested that Russia was ready for western reforms, and that had Peter employed a modicum of restraint and respected the sensibilities of his people, and if he had understood the importance of their traditions, he could have achieved his ends with far less violence.

4 Assessing Peter the Great

> **KEY ISSUE** What are the problems in assessing Peter?

Assessing Peter's reign is a complex task. There is indeed a wide range of views on him. To some he was the tsar reformer of Prokopovich – the great hero who alone had the vision, the wisdom and the strength of character to transform Russia single-handedly. To others he was the ineffective ruler of Chaadaev: he might have attempted to bring civilisation to Russia, but he was doomed to fail due to the inertia of his people and his limited understanding of his own capabilities. Others compare the cost and effectiveness of his reforms and reach their own conclusions. This latter approach – the more difficult approach – is the one the student must attempt. To do so we must penetrate the mythology of Peter's reign and the propaganda which coloured the writings of admirers and critics alike. This is no easy task. In the following chapters we shall consider the evidence, dealing especially with Peter's foreign policy, his central and local government reforms, his reforms of the economy, of education and of the Church, and consider the opposition and support he encountered.

References

1 James Cracraft (ed.), *For God and Peter the Great: the Works of Thomas Consett, 1723–29* (Columbia University Press, 1982), pp. 284–87.
2 Ian Grey, *Peter the Great: Emperor of All Russia* (Hodder & Stoughton, 1960), pp. 326–27.
3 Nicholas V. Raisanovsky, *The Image of Peter the Great in Russian History and Thought* (Oxford University Press, 1985), p. 57.
4 Ibid., p. 102.
5 Ibid., p. 143.
6 M.S. Anderson, *Peter the Great* (Thames & Hudson, 1978), p. 127.

Working on chapter I

Summary Diagram
Evolving views of Peter the Great

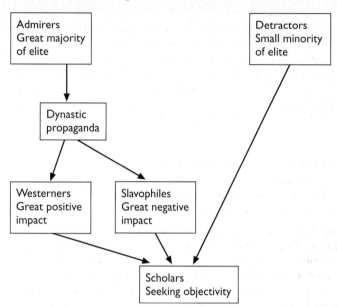

2 The Tsarist Inheritance

POINTS TO CONSIDER

What was Russia like when Peter ascended the throne? This chapter will discuss the long-standing weakness of Russia and the scale of the problems Peter faced as ruler. Try to assess what Russia's long-term problems were and how well prepared Peter was to tackle them.

KEY DATES

1672 Birth of Peter.
1676 Death of Alexei.
1682 Death of Fedor III, revolt of the *streltsy*, Peter and Ivan made co-tsars under regency of Sophia.
1687 Golitsyn's first campaign against Crimea.
1688 Golitsyn's second campaign against Crimea.
1689 Peter married to Eudoxia Lopukhina, fall of Sophia.
1690 Tsarevich Alexis born, Drunken Synod formed.
1694 Tsaritsa Natalya dies.

It is commonly assumed that seventeenth-century Russia, before Peter the Great assumed the throne, was isolated, weak and backward. The outside world knew little of it and cared less. It was a nation which could not hope to challenge its aggressive neighbours. Swedes, Poles and Crimean Tatars alike held Russia in utter contempt and enriched themselves at its expense. The arts and technology which western Europe was rapidly developing were unknown in Russia. It is central to Peter's claim to greatness that he was personally responsible for changing this. But as historians we cannot allow such assumptions to pass untested. Was Russia really in such a pathetic plight? Was Peter in any way adequately raised and educated to tackle Russia's problems? It is through such questions that we can begin to make a reasoned analysis of Peter's reign.

1 Russia's Isolation

> **KEY ISSUE** What in Russia's history and traditions separated it from the west?

a) The growth of the Russian State

It is certain that Russia before Peter the Great had experienced a great deal of isolation. Yet this had not always been the case. The first Russian state, based on Kiev, was powerful and well known from the ninth century. But impoverished by a shift in trade routes, and further weakened by wars of succession, its greatness was short-lived. In the thirteenth century Russia was easily conquered by the subdivision of the Tatar (or Mongol) empire known as the Golden Horde. This conquest was achieved with a ferocity which left an enduring impression on the Russians – a brutal reminder of the cost of weakness and division. Nor were others slow to take advantage of Russia's misfortunes. Almost immediately Swedes, Finns, Lithuanians and the Livonian and Teutonic knights attempted to seize Russian territory. Vanquished by the Tatar khans, and hemmed in by enemies to the west, the Russians went through a long period of cultural and economic isolation.

Tatar rule was not, however, disastrous for all Russians. The rulers of the small city of Moscow were quick to see the advantages to be reaped by being the most effective collaborators with their Tatar overlords. Successive Muscovite rulers won the title of 'Grand Prince' from the Tatar khans. For example, they aided a Tatar sack of the rival city of Tver. For such servility they won power and wealth, which allowed them greatly to expand the territory of Moscow, by purchase and conquest. As internal disputes weakened Tatar control, it was possible for Moscow to begin to assert its independence. In the fifteenth century the Golden Horde was fractured into the Khanates of Kazan, Astrakhan and Crimea. As a result, in 1480 Ivan III (the Great) (reigned 1462–1505) ceased paying tribute, formally ending a 'Tatar Yoke' which had been ineffective for decades. Furthermore, when Constantinople fell to the Turks, he took the opportunity to marry Sophia, the only surviving imperial princess. He also adopted the imperial emblem of the two-headed eagle. Clearly he was making a claim for the imperial status of his realm, as the inheritor of Byzantium's glory. Russia was therefore by no means short of the pretensions of power. But was there any substance to these pretensions?

The Russian army did have some successes, and Russia expanded its frontiers considerably. Ivan IV (the Dread or Terrible), who adopted the title of Tsar (or Caesar) of Russia, undertook an army reform in 1550 which saw the establishment of the *streltsy* regiments – a new elite force. His modernised army conquered the Khanates of Astrakhan and Kazan, and his successes opened the way for Russian expansion into Siberia. But for Russia the Crimean khan still remained a formidable enemy, capable of launching massive raids deep into Russian territory which carried off vast numbers of Russians into slavery. Indeed even when Peter came to the throne Russia paid the khans not to launch such raids, and the khans insisted that these payments were tribute. But it was against western European forces that Russian weakness was most obvious. When Ivan IV became embroiled in a war with Poland-Lithuania and Sweden (1558–83), he met complete and humiliating failure.

Even worse were the dreadful humiliations Russia suffered during the *Smutnoe Vremia* – the Time of Troubles (1598–1613). The extinction of the ruling dynasty, the resulting attempts by leading nobles to seize the throne, peasant revolts and the appearance of pretenders to the throne all reduced Russia to chaos. Such weakness was an invitation to Swedish and Polish intervention. The Swedes seized Novgorod, and the Poles even held the Kremlin for a time. In short, the Time of Troubles was marked by social upheaval, civil strife, serf and Cossack risings, foreign intervention, major Tatar raids, and famine – all of which nearly resulted in the extinction of the Muscovite state. The lesson was clear. Even with a strong central authority Russia could not defeat its western neighbours, and without that central authority Russia was absolutely incapable of defending itself. Furthermore the new Romanov dynasty had to make major concessions to end foreign intervention, ceding the Baltic coastline to Sweden and Smolensk to Poland – concessions which the Russians never intended to be permanent.

Tatar rule and later the powerful and hostile states on Russia's frontier did much to separate Russia from the outside world. The resulting economic and cultural isolation was intensified by religious differences. Unlike the west, the Russians had embraced the Greek Orthodox Church in the tenth century. After Constantinople fell to the Turks in the fifteenth century, Moscow began to see itself as the third, and last, Rome. With the Rome of St Peter (Rome itself) and the Rome of Constantine (Constantinople) fallen to heathens, it was held that Moscow inherited the guardianship of Christianity. It was the sole remaining bastion of the true Christian faith, and could not be replaced. The Greek Church, by being directly subject to Moslem Turkish rule, had lost much of its moral authority. To Russians the Roman Church – and later Protestant sects – were heretics who must never be allowed to corrupt the pure Russian faith. Russians believed that they – and they alone – held the true faith, and their hope of salvation depended on maintaining its purity. Any contact with heretical westerners endangered their souls. Western ideas, arts and technology were therefore automatically viewed with hostility. The Russian Orthodox Church was undoubtedly therefore a strong force of ultra-conservatism and xenophobia.

b) The first steps out of Isolation

But Russian isolation was certainly not complete. Travellers visited Russia and established commercial links which the tsars were eager to encourage. The tsars sent embassies abroad. Yet the conduct of these embassies, which were ignorant of the behaviour that western courts had come to expect, did not necessarily improve Russia's prestige. Also Russia still did not conduct permanent diplomatic relations with western powers. Nor was Russia involved in the international alliance system. The western powers did not see the need to cultivate Russia's favour. In the diplomatic settlements of the six-teenth and seventeenth centuries Russian interests went unheard and unheeded.

But if the west had little interest in Russia, there were Russians who were interested in the west. Western technology, despite its suspect origins, was too important to ignore. In 1655 tsar Alexei (r. 1645–76) recaptured Smolensk and later Kiev. These successes were, however, due more to the now terminal decline of the Polish state rather than to Russian prowess. Russian arms, furthermore, remained out-matched by the Swedes, against whom they fought yet another exhausting and completely unsuccessful war (1656–61). It was such failures which drove Russia's rulers to overcome their distaste for the west and attempt to copy its successes. Determined efforts were made to import the expertise necessary for Russia to redress its weakness: nearly 20,000 mercenaries and technical advisers were hired by Russia before Peter's reign. Alexei also expanded diplomatic and cultural contacts with the west. There were Russians sympathetic to western contacts. A few *boyars* (nobles) even adopted western fashions such as shaving, a fashion which Peter embraced as a youth. Alexei even showed a slight interest – novel for Russia – in the sea, and had a ship built, the *Orel* (Eagle), which was unfortunately destroyed soon after. Such facts are crucial evidence to those who argue that tsar Peter's later reforms were by no means revolutionary in nature.

Despite these moves, basic attitudes had not changed. Despite the influx of foreigners as advisers and mercenaries, there was still viru-lent xenophobia. Foreigners were required to live in the *nemetskaya sloboda* – the German suburb – so as not to contaminate Russians with their heretical beliefs. Nor was Russia an attractive employer to for-eigners. Even by the standards of the day, foreigners found Moscow to be crude, squalid and violent. The comments of visitors showed deep contempt for the Russians. Adam Olearius, the scholar and diplomat from Holstein, wrote of his visits during the 1630s and 1640s, in his *Voyages and Travels*, that if:

1   a man consider the natures and manner of life of the Muscovites, he will be forced to avow, that there cannot be anything more barbarous than that people. ... They never learn any art or science, nor apply them-selves to any kind of study: on the contrary, they are so ignorant, as to

5   think, a man cannot make an almanac unless he be a sorcerer, nor fore-tell the revolutions of the moon and eclipses, unless he have some com-munication with devils. ... This aversion I discovered in the Muscovites, took off that little inclination I sometime had to embrace that employ-ment, which was offered me. ...

10   They are all much given to quarrelling, insomuch that in the streets they will rail at, and abuse one another like fish-wives, and that with such animosity, that those who are not acquainted with their humour think they will not part without fighting; but they seldom come to those

extremities, or if they fight, it is with their fists ... and the height of their
15 rage is kicking, as much as they can, in the belly and about the sides.
'Twas never yet known that any Muscovite fought with sword or pistol.[1]

Furthermore, those with valuable skills, such as the Scottish mercenary General Patrick Gordon, found that they would never be per-
mitted to leave Russian service. He soon longed to leave a country
where:

1 I perceived strangers to be looked upon as a company of hirelings, and,
   at the best ... [as a necessary evil]; no honours or degrees of prefer-
   ment to be expected here but military, and that with a limited
   command, in the attainment whereof a good mediator ... and a piece
5 of money or other bribe, is more available as the merit or sufficiency
   of the person ... no marrying with natives, strangers being looked upon
   by the best sort as scarcely Christians and by plebeians as mere pagans
   ... the people being morose and niggard, and yet overweening and valu-
   ing themselves above all other nations; and worst of all, the pay small.[2]

Still, despite the difficulties, foreigners were going to Russia, and
there was a section of the Russian elite who favoured much closer contact with the west. Russia by the end of the seventeenth century was
clearly beginning to move out of its isolation.

There were also signs that Russia's diplomatic isolation may have
been drawing to a close. In 1683 the Turks undertook a disastrous
siege of Vienna. In the following years, under Polish, Venetian and
Austrian pressure, it appeared that their position in Europe could collapse totally. The Poles wanted Russian support for this war and were
prepared to offer a price which the Russians could not refuse – Kiev.
In a treaty of 1667 Russia had promised to return Kiev to Poland in
two years. It was a promise that Russia never kept. Kiev, the capital of
the first Russian state, was of so much emotional value that the
Russians could not bear to do so. Now the Poles offered to withdraw
their claims on the city if Russia went to war with the Turks and their
Crimean Tatar vassals. For the Poles this was a very heavy price to pay.
What then could Russia offer to make such a price worthwhile?
Russia, after all, had scarcely proved a formidable enemy to the Poles:
was it not too weak to prove a worthwhile ally?

2 Russia's Weakness

> **KEY ISSUES** How urgently did seventeenth-century Russia need
> western ideas and technology, and how successful were Peter's
> predecessors in gaining them?

a) Political backwardness

That Russia had been lagging behind the west in a number of areas is clear. These included political backwardness. Western Europe in the seventeenth century was no stranger to absolute monarchy. But not even Louis XIV exercised the arbitrary, despotic powers of the tsars. Even the greatest Russian *boyars* (nobles) debased themselves before the tsar and referred to themselves as his *kholops* – his slaves. In theory there were no limits to the autocratic powers of the tsar. Russia itself was seen as his *votchina* – his personal property. From the greatest to the lowest, property, privileges and even life itself depended on the whim of the tsar. There were, it is true, representative bodies within Russia. There was the *boyar duma* of the nobles and the *zemsky sobor* (assembly of the land), which included representatives from the provinces (in 1613 even some peasants). The tsar could summon and consult these bodies. Indeed, after the Time of Troubles tsar Michael consulted them frequently. But they did not develop into bodies which could curtail autocratic power. Basically, they lacked any corporate identity – their common interests were not as important to them as their differences. They never had the control over state finances which gave the English Parliament its power. They also had no conception of the growing representative bodies in the west. They therefore never sought the role of limiting the authority of the sovereign. As the Romanov dynasty became secure, they became irrelevant. The tsars remained arbitrary and despotic rulers who governed by decree.

Restraints upon the conduct of the tsars did, however, exist in the form of tradition and the Church. Elaborate and time-consuming rituals governed much of their lives. They were generally deeply pious men. Alexei spent several hours a day in prayer, and lived a life very similar to that of a monk. The tsars were certainly not above demanding 'loans' from the Church which they never repaid, nor would they tolerate criticism from the priesthood, but they were generally willing to be guided by the patriarch. At times they allowed the patriarch a status of equality with themselves. Thus this extremely conservative institution had enormous influence over the tsars. This could have its disadvantages. Alexei loyally supported Nikon, the Patriarch (1652–66), who was determined to correct a number of errors which had entered Russian liturgy and ritual during centuries of isolation, and to make Russia conform with the original Greek doctrine. Yet his arrogance alienated even the deeply pious tsar by 1658, and he lost effective power over the Church several years before he was formally deposed, but by then the damage had been done. Nikon's reforms included that Christ's name must be written as 'Iisus' instead of 'Isus', and that Russians were to cross themselves with three, instead of two, fingers. For the illiterate laity, who only participated in the religious life of the Church through its ritual, these were monstrously sacrilegious ideas – especially as they had long been told that only Russia had the pure faith. Many felt that the reforms would doom their souls. The result was a permanent schism (perhaps involving up to 20 per cent of the population) within the Church, which had made the reforms, and defiance of the state, which attempted to enforce them. These rebels were known as either the Old Believers (the *starovery*) or as schismatics (*raskolniky*). In the face of repression the Old Believers chose either mass migration to the periphery of Russia, or mass suicide (in 1684–90 alone perhaps 20,000 burned themselves to death). Subsequent attempts to suppress this defiance were all frustrated by the fanaticism of the Old Believers.

Thus in Russia constraints on the tsar were few and the highest in the land could be brought down on the tsar's whim. For the bulk of the population there was no protection from exploitation, for along with political backwardness there was a great deal of social backwardness. The condition of the peasantry had been deteriorating for some time. From the reign of Ivan IV the Russian expansion into Siberia had been causing problems for the *boyars*. Access to this new territory gave peasants the opportunity to abandon impoverished homes and uncongenial overlords for new lands. The entire economic security of the *boyars* was being undermined. This led to the first moves to impose serfdom on the peasantry – denying them the right to migrate to protect the interests of the *boyars*. Serfdom was extended in 1649 with a new legal code – the *Ulozhenie* – which gave legal status to the institution. The interests of the *boyars* were indeed being protected, but only at the price of raising severe social tensions. Serfdom was bitterly resented by the peasantry. As the revolt of Stenka Razin, which ran from 1667 to 1671, showed – attracting as it did Cossacks, fugitive serfs and slaves, non-Russians and malcontents of all kinds – these social tensions were not eased by the passage of time.

b) Economic backwardness

As is often the case, alongside political and social backwardness there was economic backwardness, with which was associated technological backwardness. Agriculture remained an extremely backward sector of the Russian economy. The best soil was in the south, the black earth of the steppe, which had been for much of Russia's history under foreign occupation, and still suffered Tatar raids. Russian agriculture mostly developed in the north, where the soil quality was poor, rainfall uncertain and the harsh climate allowed only a brief growing season. Yields were therefore low. No reliable surplus existed of a size to attract investment. Farming techniques therefore remained primitive. Ploughs which only scratched the earth instead of turning it over were the norm, as was an inefficient three-field system, by which one-third of the land lay fallow each year. At the end of Peter's reign Russia had a population of roughly 14 million, of whom 97 per cent lived in the countryside. The peasantry could, despite occasional crop failures and even famine, generally support itself. But there were, as we shall see (page 94), rigid limits to what the state could extract in taxation.

There was also absent from Russia any sign of a class which might have developed into a significant middle class or bourgeoisie. There was certainly a lot of interest in trade and manufacturing, and Russian merchants astonished foreigners with their sharp practice and dishonesty. But few could become rich through trade. If a profitable trade was developed by Russian entrepreneurs, the tsars, eager for more revenue, would declare it a royal monopoly. The crown, for example, made royal monopolies on trade in a long list of goods including cereals, vodka, caviar and leather. Such merchants who still managed to earn great wealth would often be conscripted into the ranks of the *gosti*, an honoured merchant class – in short made servants to the crown and dependent upon royal favour. Nor was there much opportunity for the development of an independent and wealthy class of manufacturers. There was plenty of activity in manufacturing. The limitations of agriculture required many Russians to supplement their income through activities such as leather tanning, weaving and distilling salt. Thus a great volume of manufacturing took place, but it remained very small scale and primitive: cottage industries and tiny workshops supplied the limited needs of the locality. What little larger scale production existed, which until the seventeenth centuries was largely limited to iron, salt and coarse cloth, was again controlled by the tsar.

c) Attempts to remedy Russia's backwardness

But just as the tsars had been unable to avoid accepting the superiority of western military expertise, so they were driven to accept that western technology and industry were an essential part of that superiority. They realised that they must establish the industries needed to complement their military reforms. Thus in 1632 western experts established iron works at Tula in the Urals. When Peter was born in 1672, 20 small private and state-owned iron foundries existed in Russia. Thus Russia had taken its first faltering steps in the direction of industrialisation before his succession. But these steps were noteworthy especially for the almost complete absence of Russian capital, management and skilled workforce. If Russia was to address its economic and technological backwardness, a truly enormous amount of work remained to be done.

While it is, therefore, realistic to speak of Russia's isolation, weakness and backwardness, it is still clear that these problems were not as great as they had been by the time Peter came to the throne. In most areas the reform of Russia had begun – even if only in the most tentative manner. If Russia was to benefit from the efforts of his predecessors, the new tsar would have to press on with this process of reform. It remains to be seen how well suited Peter was to bear such a responsibility.

3 Peter's Early Years

> **KEY ISSUE** How well prepared was Peter to meet the
> responsibilities of the tsar?

Peter was born on 30 May 1672, a child of tsar Alexei's second marriage. Alexei's first wife, Maria Miloslavskaya, gave him eight daughters, but only two sons survived, Fedor and Ivan. They were both extremely sickly and unlikely to live long. His second wife, Natalya Naryshkina, gave him a much more robust son. Peter eventually grew to six foot seven inches in height, though he was slimly built. Alexei clearly had great hopes for his youngest son. But he did not live to see them fulfilled, as he died suddenly in 1676. Because of this Peter was to have a most unusual upbringing. Whether this was to his advantage or disadvantage is a matter of debate.

Peter's standard of education can be questioned. With Alexei's death this became the responsibility of his half-brother, the physically weak and semi-invalid Fedor III (r. 1676–82). Fedor treated his half-brother generously enough. He chose as Peter's tutor Nikita Zotov, a devout man who was knowledgeable of the Bible. But he was no scholar and was perhaps ill-suited to his role. Zotov, it is clear, allowed his pupil to follow his own inclinations in the subjects which interested him, rather than insisting on the discipline of a formal education. In contrast, Sweden's Charles XII, following the common practice of the time, underwent a carefully planned education specifically designed to prepare him for the throne. In later life Peter was to be aware of the limitations of his education; his handwriting remained poor, and his spelling and grammar haphazard. Throughout his life, furthermore, he showed a preference for the immediately useful and practical: arguably he lacked the intellectual training to visualise clearly either what he wanted Russia to become or how he could implement such a transformation.

Fedor's death in 1682 led to a great upheaval in Peter's life. There were two possible candidates for the throne. Peter's elder half-brother, Ivan, was sixteen years old, but he was severely handicapped. Alternatively there was the obviously robust and intelligent nine year old Peter. The Patriarch, Joachim, hastily convened a *sobor* (assembly) from those present in Moscow, and urged Peter's preference. Peter was thus acclaimed tsar by a crowd assembled in Red Square. His mother, Natalya, was to be regent. But his half-sister, Sophia, was not prepared to see Ivan's rights ignored. Her own position was, after all, at risk: as the tsar's unwanted half-sister she could easily find herself forced into a nunnery. At 25 Sophia was intelligent, ambitious and decisive, and for a woman of the period unusually well educated. In an age where women of the royal family were confined to the *terem* her achievements were truly astonishing. She was certainly ruthless

-*Profile*-

Sophia (1657–1704), regent of Russia from 1682 until 1689. The eldest daughter of tsar Alexei, she had an unusually wide education which set her eyes beyond the *terem* (secluded women's quarters). Strong-willed, intelligent and ambitious, when her brother, tsar Fedor, died in 1682 she assumed the leadership of the Miloslavsky faction at court, opposing the Naryshkins, who championed Peter's claim to the throne. She triumphed over the Naryshkins by inciting the *streltsy* into revolt. When the *streltsy* stormed into the Kremlin, a terrified Peter witnessed the brutality with which many Naryshkins were murdered. At Sophia's instigation the *streltsy* demanded that Ivan and Peter reign jointly, with Sophia as regent.

Sophia proved a competent regent, and was ably guided by a *boyar* with a western outlook, Vasily Golitsyn, whom she took as a lover. She brought the *streltsy* to heel, promoted industry and attracted more foreigners to Russia. She had, in fact, quite ambitious plans for reform in Russia, but was too cautious to challenge the traditionalists openly. In international affairs she concluded the treaty of Nerchinsk (1689) with China, setting Russia's eastern frontier on the Amur river. She also concluded an agreement with Poland, gaining Kiev permanently for Russia and joining in the coalition including Austria, Venice and Poland against the Turks. The dismal failure of two campaigns against the Turks' Crimean vassals undermined her position. When Peter challenged her authority, her support evaporated. She was confined in the Novodevichy convent, and in 1698 was forced to become a nun. As long as she lived Peter feared she would challenge his position once again.

and courageous enough to seize the chance to challenge Peter's succession.

This opportunity was offered by the *streltsy*, the musketeer corps of Ivan IV, of whom there were about 22,000 in Moscow. As their elite status and privileges were undermined, their discipline and reliability had deteriorated. There were clear signs of unrest in their ranks. Sophia's agents began to stir them up, spreading rumours that Fedor had been poisoned and Ivan's life was in peril at the hands of Natalya's family, the Naryshkins, whom Sophia was determined to destroy. In May 1682 the *streltsy* mutinied. They invaded the Kremlin to annihilate the Naryshkins. In desperation Natalya appeared before the *streltsy* with both Peter and Ivan, in an attempt to calm the mutineers by showing that both were unharmed. But the *streltsy* had already gone too far to draw back. All that Natalya's stratagem achieved was to provide Peter with a close view of the brutal murder of Natalya's family and supporters, as the mutineers rampaged through the Kremlin, seeking his relatives to massacre. Subsequently, when the *streltsy* demanded that henceforth Peter and Ivan must reign jointly (Ivan remained co-tsar until he died in 1696), with Sophia as regent, nobody had the courage to object. This terrifying experience had a massive impact on Peter. According to Robert Massie, he grew to hate Moscow and the Kremlin. He was eventually to turn his back on the city and build an entirely new capital – St Petersburg (see page 66).

4 Growing up at Preobrazhenskoe

KEY ISSUE How did Peter learn to despise traditional Russia?

More than causing him to detest the Kremlin, the traumatic events of 1682 also severed Peter from the bonds of ritual and tradition which might otherwise have shaped his reign. For despite the horrors he had seen, for Peter the *coup* had one favourable result: he was no longer wanted at the centre of government. He therefore had far more personal freedom than he would otherwise have enjoyed. Natalya chose to live away from the Kremlin, preferring Alexei's hunting lodge at Preobrazhenskoe outside Moscow. There Peter indulged in games and sought his pleasures far from the constraints normal to his rank. But he retained the material advantages of that rank. He enjoyed playing soldiers, but he was not limited to toys. He drew into his games the children of nobles sent to be his companions, and later increased their numbers by recruiting servants. He also drew muskets and even cannon from the state armoury. In short, he raised what became regular regiments, which lived and trained as professional soldiers. Thus was founded the Preobrazhensky and later the Semyonovsky Guards. Rather than be their commander, however, Peter enlisted as a drummer boy, later promoting himself to a bombardier. Massie and others see this as Peter early setting the pattern which he would follow all his life – learning each trade from the bottom and insisting on promotion through merit, not birth. But equally it was a way of avoiding responsibility.

Preobrazhenskoe gave Peter a great deal of undisciplined freedom. It allowed him to develop his own hobbies, which included crafts, such as joinery, woodturning and stonemasonry – strictly practical skills which were very unlikely interests for a future tsar. Indeed, by the standards of the age, they were highly unsuitable interests for a youth supposedly being prepared to rule a vast nation. This freedom also gave him far more contact with foreigners from the German suburb than he would otherwise have enjoyed. In 1688 he developed an interest in the workings of a sextant, and a Dutch merchant was recruited to teach him the arithmetic and geometry necessary to use it. He also developed a most un-Russian fascination with boats – reputedly after seeing an old English built boat. For Peter sailing and shipbuilding became a major passion. But this alarmed his mother, who like most Russians found ships both alien and frightening. Nor did she approve of his association with heretical foreigners. Clearly, he was developing attitudes and interests such as no tsar had ever held before. He had never learned adoration of tradition, unquestioned devotion to the Russian faith, or assumptions of Russian superiority in all things – in fact the basic attitudes of his predecessors. Russia's isolation, weakness and backwardness, which they had reluctantly accepted and attempted to redress, were glaringly obvious to Peter, and he viewed them with a sense of urgency which they had lacked.

In 1689 Natalya arranged his marriage with Eudoxia Lopukhina, to distract him from such interests. His marriage also signalled that the regency must be drawing to a close. After all, a nine year old boy needed a regent, but Peter was now 17 and married. Sophia had held power capably, but her office was limited to Peter's childhood. Her position was weakening. It was also undermined by the failures of her foreign policy. In return for permanent title to the city of Kiev, Sophia agreed to join a coalition with Austria, Poland and Venice determined to drive the Turks from Europe (see page 19). To this end she sent two expeditions (1688 and 1689) against the Crimean Tatars, who were Turkish vassals. Large, but ill-prepared and unenthusiastic Russian armies marched south. Both campaigns were reduced to a shambles when the Tatars burned the pasture ahead of the Russians, which was vital to feed their horses. Their withdrawal was chaotic. Sophia's attempts to disguise a disaster as a victory cost her support, and Peter's initial refusal to receive Golitsyn (her lover and military commander) to bestow upon him the rewards for his 'victory' increased the tension at court.

The breach between regent and tsar was becoming open, and it became obvious that a storm was brewing at court. The crisis came on 17 August 1689. Sophia ordered a large *streltsy* escort to conduct her to the Donskoy monastery, but supporters of Peter mistakenly assumed she intended an attack on Preobrazhenskoe. Peter was warned of this in the middle of the night and fled in terror (leaving behind his wife and his mother) to the Troitsky monastery – the traditional sanctuary of the tsars in times of great danger. By fleeing to such an impregnable and sacred place, Peter had put himself in a strong position. He was announcing that he was repudiating Sophia's regency because his life was threatened, and from a place of safety he could and did force religious, civil and military leaders to make a choice – between supporting a regent whose regency would end soon anyway and a tsar who would soon be in a position to take revenge on those who defied him. Sophia's support collapsed as *streltsy* officers, Patriarch Joachim, foreign officers led by General Gordon and other officials hurriedly went to Troitsky to assure the tsar of their loyalty. Her remaining handful of supporters were soon either exiled or executed. Furious but helpless, Sophia was forced to obey Peter's orders sending her to Novodevichy convent – a comfortable prison, but a prison nonetheless. Ivan, whom Peter personally liked, and who was willing to follow Peter's lead, remained as co-tsar. But the regency was over.

5 Archangel and the German Suburb

> **KEY ISSUE** Why did Peter have such unorthodox pastimes and interests?

Though Peter (now aged 17) had ended the regency, he was in no hurry to take up the reins of government himself. He was happy to leave his mother – far less competent than Sophia – in charge of the government, while his half-brother and co-tsar, Ivan, performed the ceremonial duties of that office. His wife, whom he had married obediently enough, meant little to him. After the birth of his son, Alexis, he simply ignored her existence. Still determined to avoid responsibility, he clung to the undisciplined freedom he had enjoyed at Preobrazhenskoe. He returned to his boats and his soldiers, organising large-scale military manoeuvres, and he also indulged a sometimes dangerous passion for firework displays. In fact his pastimes became increasingly unorthodox and blatant, especially his interest in foreigners and their ways, much to the horror of many Russians. He grew to prefer the hospitality and easy-going company found in the German suburb, where the carousing, drinking and dancing offered a stark contrast to the elaborate ritual of the Kremlin. He befriended the old Scottish mercenary, General Gordon, and formed a very close friendship with a Swiss adventurer, Franz Lefort. He even went to the lengths of wearing western clothes and taking a German woman as his mistress.

His bizarre entertainments were to horrify his subjects even more. A group of kindred spirits, foreign and Russian, known originally as the 'Jolly Company', had coalesced around Peter. Up to 200 might gather together for gargantuan eating and drinking bouts lasting for days. Peter chose to organise this company into a parody of the court: the 'All-Joking, All-Drunken Synod of Fools and Jesters', dedicated to drinking, buffoonery and masquerade. The Drunken Synod had regular rituals and rites, and a strict hierarchy, with Prince Fedor Romodanovsky being the 'Prince-Caesar', to whom Peter (who again awarded himself only modest rank) afforded the most elaborate reverence. With his old tutor, Zotov, given the title of 'Prince-Pope', the Drunken Synod did more than parody the court: it went out of its way to mock the Church, regularly offending foreigner and Russian alike with its irreverent, if not blasphemous, conduct. The Austrian diplomat, Korb, later described a procession of the Drunken Synod through Moscow:

1   He that bore the assumed honours of the Patriarch [Zotov] was conspicuous in the vestments proper to a bishop. Bacchus was decked with a mitre, and went stark naked, to betoken lasciviousness to the lookers on. Cupid and Venus were the insignia on his crozier [Bishop's staff],
5   lest there should be any mistake about what flock he was pastor of. The remaining rout of Bacchanalians came after him, some carrying great bowls full of wine, others mead, others again beer and brandy. ... Two of those pipes through which some people are pleased to puff smoke ... being set crosswise, served the scenic bishop to confirm the rites of
10 consecration. Now, who would believe that the sign of the cross – that most precious pledge of our redemption – was held up to mockery?[3]

Peter went to immense trouble organising the Drunken Synod's activities in detail, and he maintained such interests throughout his life. Why he did so is far from clear. Perhaps amusement was his only motive. As Kliuchevsky wrote, Peter had 'such a sense of his own importance that he paid no attention whatever to the elementary rules of behaviour'.[4] He simply did not care who was offended by his revelries. Or perhaps there was a political or educational motive: by such mockery he was offering a challenge to the intense conservatism of the Russians and their Church. Peter was personally deeply devout, but he unquestionably saw the Russian Orthodox Church as a backward-looking and insular institution, whose ultra-conservative influence he resented. In the final analysis, Peter certainly enjoyed the Drunken Synod, or he would not have taken such pains for so long with it, and its offensiveness to conservatives, especially within the Church, was part of the pleasure, but there is scant evidence to suggest that he had any deeper motive.

Peter also indulged his passion for ships, in 1693 visiting Archangel on the White Sea, Russia's only important port and point of contact with the west. He had promised Natalya not to sail on the sea, but on arrival he went straight to his new, specially built, 12-gun yacht, *St Peter*, impatient to test her. He commanded her as part of the escort for an English and Dutch convoy of merchant ships when it departed from Archangel. He enjoyed himself immensely; in his own words he 'was much delighted with his voyage, so much at large, but did not stop here, and therefore bent his thoughts wholly towards building a fleet.'[5] Soon he was ambitious to command larger ships, commanding that one be built in Archangel, and also ordered a frigate from Amsterdam. Despite the personal tragedy of his mother's death in February 1694 Peter returned to Archangel that summer. His new ships, the *St Paul*, and the Dutch frigate *Holy Prophecy*, delighted him. Now commanding a tiny flotilla, he raised a number of his comrades – who were totally ignorant of the sea – to the rank of Admiral. He awarded himself the rank of skipper, of which he was immensely proud. He was now 22, and with the death of his mother he was even less restrained in his conduct and ceased to take part in the traditional rituals expected of a tsar. But he could no longer avoid the duty of actually ruling. Russia was facing pressing problems, not least the still unresolved war against the Crimean Tatars. The year 1694, in fact, marked the beginnings of his personal rule.

6 Conclusion

> **KEY ISSUE** Was Peter adequately prepared to meet Russia's needs?

We have seen that Russia at the end of the seventeenth century was a nation with severe problems which its rulers were attempting to address. Steps were being taken to end its economic, cultural and diplomatic isolation. High priority was given to remedying its military weakness. The first steps had been taken in curing its economic and technological backwardness, though its political and social backwardness went largely unrecognised and ignored. But how significant were these steps? Russia was a vast land, its people and institutions were xenophobic and ultra-conservative. Could importing a handful of foreign mercenaries and technicians amongst perhaps 14 million Russians around 1700, and building a score of iron foundries, signal the start of an irreversible, fundamental transformation of Russia? Or was something more drastic required? It is important to recognise that Russia had progressed under Peter's predecessors, but it is equally important to recognise the colossal scale of the changes which would still be required if Russia was ever to deal with the west as an equal.

Was Peter a ruler capable of offering something more drastic? His education was limited, his emotional stability questionable. His youth was spent in irresponsible pleasure-seeking, and his pastimes were hardly those which would prepare him for his great responsibilities. In his later teens he lived a wild, debauched life, and cared nothing for those he offended. Yet perhaps his unconventional upbringing was a greater asset than it seems. Was it not perhaps more important for Russia to have a ruler unconstrained by the traditions and rituals which had bound his predecessors, than it was for

him to have the benefits of a formal education? Did not his unconventional life-style, with his close association with foreigners, give
him a clearer impression how poorly Russia compared with the west
than his predecessors ever had? He certainly developed a burning,
ruthless determination to reshape Russia, and he would brook no
protests from traditionalists. He also showed a capacity for savagery
when faced with defiance or revolt. This might explain his brutal
treatment of his son, Alexis (see page 106). But he was never given
to the unrestrained terrorism of Ivan the Dread. He grew into a man
of towering drive, endless curiosity and boundless energy which
made him unable to stay still anywhere for long. He also grew into a
man so driven by his own dreams for Russia that he never understood, much less sympathised with, those who were offended or
harmed in the process. Peter certainly had his limitations, but he
also had his strengths, and as historians we must recognise and
acknowledge both.

Even at this early stage we can see that the life and age of
Peter the Great can be interpreted in a number of ways. We shall
see the debates increase as his personal rule progressed. As we
address the great developments of his reign – his political, economic and social reforms, and the successes and failures of his
foreign policy – we shall be asking questions about how fundamentally he actually changed Russia, and whether these changes
were worth the immense price paid. But we shall also have to bear
in mind the issues raised in this chapter: about how much of the
groundwork for his reforms had been laid by his predecessors,
and whether he really had the genius and vision to change such a
vast nation single-handedly.

References

1 Basil Dmytryshyn (ed.), *Medieval Russia: a Source Book, 900–1700* (Holt,
  Rinehart & Winston, 1967), pp. 236–37.
2 General Patrick Gordon, *Pages from the Diary of General Patrick Gordon of
  Auchleuchries in the Years 1635–1699* (Frank Cass & Co. Ltd., 1968), 9
  September 1661, p. 47.
3 Johann-Georg Korb, *Diary of an Austrian Secretary of Legation at the Court of
  Czar Peter the Great* (Frank Cass & Co. Ltd., 1968), p. 255.
4 Vasili Klyuchevsky, *Peter the Great* (Macmillan & Co. Ltd., 1963), p. 35.
5 James Cracraft (ed.), *For God and Peter the Great: the Works of Thomas Consett,
  1723–29* (Columbia University Press, 1982), p. 213.

Working on chapter 2

Summary Diagram
Influences on the young Peter

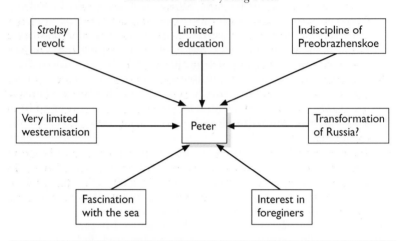

Source-based questions on Chapter 2

1 Two foreigners' views on Russian barbarity
Read the extracts from Olearius and Gordon on pages 13–14 and answer the following questions:

a) What were the main reasons why Russian customs were so alien to the westerners? (*6 marks*)
b) In what ways had both been most offended by Russians? (*6 marks*)
c) Explain Olearius' contempt because 'Twas never yet known that any Muscovite fought with sword or pistol' (lines 15–16). (*4 marks*)
d) Why did Gordon accept Russian service, when he so obviously resented his poor pay? (*4 marks*)

Hints and advice: Questions of this type are very common in examinations, and it is worthwhile to take some pains in practising answering them. Be sure to read the sources carefully a number of times. Consider who wrote them, and in what circumstances they were written. Are there any grounds to suggest prejudice by the authors? Use your knowledge of the period to put them in context and interpret them. Take your time and give a carefully considered answer. Remember, examiners are impressed by quality more than quantity. Also, as with any examination question, be sure that you are answering the question as set.

a) An obvious point is the xenophobia we know existed in Russia. Why did it exist and what were the consequences of Russia's long isolation and backwardness? Consider also that Moscow was held to be the third Rome – how would this influence the Russians' conduct towards foreigners?

b) Remember, they were both well travelled men with a strong sense of their own worth. But they came to Russia for different reasons. Olearius the envoy was a scholar, and was proud of the fact. Gordon the mercenary had what was seen at the time as an honourable profession. Both had it clearly in mind how they expected to be treated by the peoples they visited. In what ways were they disappointed?

c) Consider what you know about Europe in this period. How would a German expect honourable people to settle serious disputes? Remember that the duelling code was still held strongly in the west. How would we expect him to view people who fought in the street with their fists and boots?

d) Remember that the tsars needed foreign mercenaries, but frequently lacked the money to pay them. Yet they had no intention of losing the services of foreigners. What choices would be left to Gordon if he was forbidden to leave Russia and ordered to serve in the tsar's army? What legal recourse did he have?

From Azov to Narva: the First Steps in Foreign Policy

3

POINTS TO CONSIDER

This chapter will introduce you to Peter's first steps in foreign policy. Your aim should be to understand precisely what he hoped to achieve. Study the maps and familiarise yourself with the territory Peter wanted to win, and try to assess how formidable were the powers Peter challenged. What, if anything, did he achieve with his early foreign policy? Did he lay the groundwork here for his recovery from the battle of Narva?

KEY DATES

1695 March	First Azov campaign begins.
1696 May	Second Azov campaign begins.
1697 March 20	Great Embassy departs.
1700 August 9	Great Northern War begins.
1700 November 20	Battle of Narva.

The failure of the expeditions Sophia sent against the Crimea (see page 21) show how weak Russia was. Few therefore could expect much success from a young, headstrong tsar such as Peter. Yet his claim to greatness is based to a large extent upon his foreign policy. In this chapter we shall consider his early moves in this field and see if we can find within them evidence of clear vision in his aims and a sense of realism in his policies. His initial failure and subsequent success against the Turkish fortress of Azov (1695–96), his much celebrated Great Embassy to the west (March 1697–September 1698), his entry into the Great Northern War and terrible humiliation at the battle of Narva (20 November 1700), provide ample material with which we can discuss such questions. He fought formidable enemies, but they did have their problems – the Turks were distracted by a major war with the Austrians, and the powerful Swedish army was supported by strictly limited reserves of manpower. We must therefore ask whether Peter aimed for objectives which were both achievable and worth the resources which were expended on reaching them.

1 The Azov Campaigns

> **KEY ISSUES** Were Peter's first campaigns amateurish and inept, and were they a valuable education in military realities?

In 1695 Peter finally turned his attention to the war against the Ottoman Turks and their Crimean vassals, begun by Sophia in 1687. Since Sophia's fall the Russians had ceased fighting the war, but the Tatars had not. They once again raided deep into Russia, carrying off thousands into slavery. Peter could not concentrate on his own amusements and ignore such raids indefinitely. In addition, he had other reasons to act. His Polish allies were threatening to conclude a separate peace with the Turks, which would humiliatingly ignore Russia's questionable contribution to the war. A campaign would also provide Peter with the chance to put his warlike games into practice. Perhaps he expected to repeat on a larger scale the easy victories of his manoeuvres at Preobrazhenskoe (see page 20). It is also clear that he wanted a fleet and intended to win an outlet to a sea which would justify one. Yet were the immense resources he committed to his campaigns in the south largely wasted? Or should they be seen as a vital step in Russia's inexorable march south? As in many of Peter's actions, the relative costs and benefits are often not easy to measure.

Peter launched his first campaign against the Turks in March 1695. This consisted of two elements. Firstly a traditional Russian army of peasant levies, 120,000 strong, under the command of Boris Sheremetev, advanced down the river Dnieper, attacking the fortifications along the way (see the map on page 31). This was really a diversion for a more modern force of 31,000 troops, which attacked the Turkish garrison town of Azov on the river Don. To the Turks this was a vital strategic position, defending their northern frontier and protecting their communications with the Caucasus. But under pressure from western Europe they had been forced to leave it nearly defenceless. Yet in reality how modern was this Russian force? Peter had his Guards Regiments and numbers of western-trained troops, but the *streltsy* (the obsolete musketeers) were still necessary to make up numbers. Predictably the outdated *streltsy*, who hated the western officers and were unwilling to obey their orders, were of little use. As so often before the Russians were further hampered by a totally inadequate supply organisation and insufficient engineers. Also this army was led by a command divided between Lefort, Gordon and Fedor Golovin. With them went the tsar, but only in the role of Bombardier Peter. The three commanders did not work well together. Peter was present, and had to be consulted on major decisions, but he was not there as tsar, and therefore the expedition lacked clear leadership. This boded ill for the campaign. It soon became clear, furthermore, that the force was too small to surround the town completely and was not equipped to prevent supplies and reinforcements reaching the town by ship.

The Russians were soon facing a failure as complete as the two campaigns of Sophia's regency. Yet Peter refused to accept this – perhaps the comparison was too humiliating for him. He overrode the experienced judgement of Gordon and agreed to a reckless frontal assault on the town. The result was predictable: 1,500 died pointlessly. That evening there 'was nothing to be seen but angry looks and sad countenances'.[1] A second attack fared no better, and the siege was abandoned. Harried by the Tatars, and with heavy rain and swollen rivers hampering their withdrawal, the Russian retreat was disastrous. Like Sophia, Peter tried to pass off defeat as victory with a triumphal entry into Moscow. He deceived no one. To add insult to injury, Sheremetev's outdated force had done quite well, capturing four Turkish fortresses along the river Dnieper.

Peter was, however, about to display one of the most valuable of his characteristics – his absolute refusal to allow even the most humiliating failure to discourage him. He also displayed a less laudable trait – his refusal to allow the cost to his nation to restrain his actions. He decided on a second, even more costly, campaign against Azov in 1696. He also showed himself willing to learn from his mistakes. This time he appointed a single commander, Alexei Shein. He also recruited more engineers and built a larger army of 46,000 Russians and 23,000 irregular Cossack and Kalmyk cavalry. Crucially he had over 20 galleys and a host of transport barges built during the winter at Voronezh on the river Don. The tsar had ruthlessly conscripted materials and unskilled peasant labourers, and had even worked on the ships himself to ensure their completion. With them the Russians cut Azov off from outside help. This time the town fell after a relatively short siege and fewer than 300 Russians died. It was Russia's first victory since Alexei's reign, and it was a victory – against the Turks – over a truly formidable, if distracted, power.

Russia finally had access to the sea in the south. But it was access only to the Azov Sea – the Turkish fortress of Kerch still blocked Russian entry into the Black Sea. Nevertheless, with a naval base established at nearby Tagenrog, Peter was determined to have a fleet. Labour and wealth were again ruthlessly conscripted, as great landowners, the Church and merchants were made responsible for constructing and fitting out ships. With great cost and labour, and much waste, they were constructed. But was the cost and effort worthwhile? They were often not good ships. As an English observer later commented, 'little is to be said in favour of [them] ... to pass them by in silence is the highest compliment'.[2] There was also the problem of the almost complete absence of Russians capable of sailing them. However, Peter had an answer to this. In November 1696 he ordered 50 men, mostly sons of nobles, to go to western Europe. They went at their own expense, and, as Orthodox Russians, at risk to

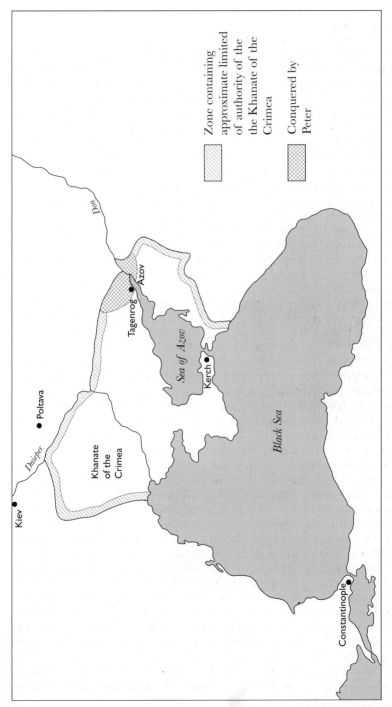

The Azov Campaigns.

their souls from contamination from western heretics. They were forbidden to return until they had mastered seamanship, navigation and
shipbuilding. Many more were to follow.

Yet what was the value of Peter's 'successes' in the south? Azov had
been taken but only at immense cost. Peter had established a fleet of
sorts. But its purpose was unclear. Was it simply to satisfy Peter's burning desire for one? The existence of a Russian fleet at Tagenrog was
certainly a source of concern to the Turks. But as long as they held
Kerch – which the Russians had no hope of capturing – the Russians
were trapped in the Sea of Azov. Was dominating such a small and isolated sea worth the resources which Peter had committed? Russia had
been glad to celebrate a rare victory but, unless that victory could be
exploited, had Russia won anything of value? As we shall see (page
55), Azov was not in Russian hands for very long but no one could
know this in 1696. Was it conceivable that Azov might have become a
base from which Russia could continue its march to the Black Sea,
and the resources Peter had committed to the area a shrewd investment for the future?

2 The Great Embassy

> **KEY ISSUE** Did the Great Embassy achieve anything more than
> providing Peter with a long holiday?

If Russia could not take Kerch alone, could it realistically look to the
west for help? For Peter to send a large embassy to the west to this end
made sense. But Russia was appalled, and Europe stunned, when it
was realised that Peter not only intended to accompany the embassy,
but to accompany it *incognito*. (In fact his anonymous status proved to
be a flimsy fiction – he took full advantage of his rank whenever he
chose, but still insisted on the privacy and freedom to pursue his own
interests, indifferent to the considerable problems of protocol this
caused for his hosts, who were baffled how to treat him.) In an age
when monarchs, unless they were in personal command of their
armies, tended not to be widely travelled, for Peter to leave his country
for a long time (he was gone 18 months) was seen as at least eccentric.
Nevertheless the embassy departed from Russia in March 1697. It was
accompanied by 'Peter Mikhailov', who was not officially referred to
as the tsar. The embassy travelled through Swedish-held Riga on the
Baltic coast to Prussia, across Germany to the Netherlands, and on to
England. From there they went to Vienna. Rushing home to deal with
a new *streltsy* mutiny, and abandoning plans to visit Venice, Peter still
found time to visit Poland's new king, Augustus.

His motives for making this journey were much discussed then and
since. Russia had long been too isolated and insignificant for the west

to worry about its needs. Possibly he thought that his presence would strengthen negotiations for western help against the Turks. But while he certainly raised this question with the leaders he met, by and large he left the matter in the hands of the official leaders of the embassy. His burning desire to see for himself the wealth and power, and the science and technology, of the west is unquestioned. He was also eager to improve his own practical skills – he spent several months working in shipyards in England and the Netherlands as a shipwright, much to the bewilderment of his hosts, who were baffled that a monarch would interest himself in such things. Also the embassy hired technical experts and purchased technology needed by Russia. But did Peter really feel that these were the proper interests of a tsar – the best way in which he could fulfil his duties? Perhaps his real motive was simpler. Just as when he assumed only junior rank in his enterprises, he was evading responsibility. It is possible that he privately saw the Great Embassy as an extended holiday.

The Great Embassy was successful in its search for technical experts and technology. The Russians, aided by their host governments, hired over 800 specialists – many of them naval officers, shipwrights and engineers. The technology they purchased included modern muskets and ring bayonets. These were the latest weapons, which allowed the muskets to continue firing while the bayonets fended off enemy cavalry, making the infantry a far more powerful and offensive force than the *streltsy* – Russia's obsolete infantry formations of musketeers who had to be protected by pikemen. Western powers also agreed to receive more Russians to be taught seafaring skills. Though puzzled by Peter's private pursuit of technical skills, his hosts were happy to assist him – hopes for commercial advantages were a strong motive. But his willingness to work with his hands was not Peter's only characteristic which surprised his hosts. His erratic conduct caused much comment at the time and subsequently. Despite his *incognito* status he did not hesitate to act like an eastern despot. He ordered that two Russians be executed in the Netherlands, much to the embarrassment of his hosts, whose laws could not permit it. In England his visit was notable for the massive vandalism his party committed on the house of the diarist John Evelyn, whose steward famously referred to the Russian party as 'right nasty'.[3]

Others were more ambivalent. Princess Sophia of Hanover, who dined with him one evening, wrote that Peter was:

1 very tall, his features are fine, and his figure very noble. He has great vivacity of mind, and a ready and just repartee. But, considering all the advantages with which nature has endowed him, it could be wished that his manners were less rustic. ... He was very merry, very talkative, and
5 we established a great friendship for each other. ... He told us that he worked himself in building ships, showed us his hands, and made us touch the callous places that had been caused by work. ... He is a very

extraordinary man. It is impossible to describe him, or even to give an idea of him. ... He has a very good heart and remarkably noble senti-
10 ments. I must tell you, also, that he did not get drunk in our presence, but we had hardly left, when the people of his suite made ample amends.[4]

John Perry, an English engineer whom Peter hired during his visit to England, wrote how he was:

1 shewn both Houses of Parliament when they were sitting, and was pre-vail'd upon to go once or twice to the play, but that was what he did not like. He spent most of his time in what related to war and shipping, and upon the water. He often took the carpenter's tools in his hands,
5 and often work'd himself in Deptford Yard, as he had done before in Holland. He would sometimes be at the smith's and sometimes at the gun-founder's, and there was scarce any art or mechanick trade what-soever, from the watch-maker to the coffin-maker, but he more or less inspected it, and even caused a model of an English coffin to be sent to
10 Russia, as he did also in many other things. Whilst he was in England he us'd to dress after the English fashion, sometimes as a gentleman, and sometimes as a seaman.[5]

Diplomatically the Great Embassy was largely a failure. If Peter hoped that he could win support – especially from the English, the Dutch and the Austrians – for his war with the Turks he was to be frus-trated. The west had its own preoccupations, centred on the ambi-tions of Louis XIV of France, not the Ottoman sultan. With the ageing and childless Charles II of Spain favouring a Bourbon heir, an already powerful and feared France stood to grow even more dominant. It was feared that a huge united European power might emerge, con-sisting of France and Spain, with much of modern Italy and Belgium and parts of Germany, ruling the combined Spanish and French col-onial empires. One general European war over the issue was just ending (the War of the League of Augsburg, 1688–97), which had failed to settle the issue. The European powers were already prepar-ing for another general war (the War of the Spanish Succession was in fact fought 1701–13). Against such a background the claims of Russia counted for little. England, the Netherlands and the Austrian Habsburgs wanted an end to the distracting war against the Turks, and they would have preferred Russia to make peace also, but this was not essential to them. In reality Peter could offer nothing to persuade the west to take Russian aspirations into account. He soon learned that his Polish, Austrian and Venetian allies intended to make peace, and that Russia must either make the best terms it could or fight on alone – an obviously hopeless proposition.

The Great Embassy proved to be extremely costly, but it had posi-tive results. Peter hired specialists, purchased technology and met some of the most powerful rulers of western Europe. In the west bewil-derment at his coarse conduct and interests was tempered by a degree of admiration for his insatiable curiosity. But was the great impact his visit made upon Peter even more important? It is generally agreed that the prosperity, the architecture, arts, libraries and scientific achievements he saw confirmed all of his impressions of Russia's backwardness and weakness. His determination to transform Russia was stiffened even more. There was perhaps one further consequence of greater significance. One foreign policy success Peter enjoyed was to ensure the election of his preferred candidate, Augustus, Elector of Saxony, to the Polish throne. On his journey home the two met. Fatefully they discussed the opportunities presented by the apparent weakness of Sweden, whose new king, Charles XII, was only 15 years old. Both nations had long held designs on Sweden's Baltic empire, and the idea was raised that the time had come to act together to break Sweden's power. There was no formal agreement but both monarchs understood that an anti-Swedish alliance might easily be reached.

-Profile-

Augustus II, elector of Saxony (r. 1694–1733) and king of Poland (r. 1696–1704 and 1709–33). The hereditary elector of Saxony, he gained the elective throne of Poland by converting to Catholicism and by securing Russian support. As king of Poland he concluded the war with the Ottoman empire, begun in 1683, with the treaty of Karlowitz (1699). By the terms of this treaty Poland gained much territory. Augustus, however, had much wider ambitions. He aimed to conquer the former Polish territory of Livonia from Sweden and add it to his hereditary Saxon domain. He would then offer the land to Poland in exchange for his Polish crown becoming hereditary. To this end he joined a coalition with Denmark and Russia aimed at conquering the Swedish Baltic empire and dividing the spoils.

In fact his Saxon army proved no match for the Swedes. The Saxons were repeatedly defeated, but Charles XII proved unable to gain a decisive victory. In 1704 the Poles, their land devastated by the war and desperate to rid themselves of foreign troops, formally deposed Augustus. It was only when Charles occupied Saxony in 1706, however, that Augustus was forced to accept the loss of his Polish throne. Yet after the Russian victory of Poltava (1709), he regained it with Russian help. He ultimately failed to make himself the hereditary king of Poland, and his reign in fact did much to bring about the final decline of Poland as a European power.

3 The Great Northern War

> **KEY ISSUES** How reckless and irresponsible was Peter's decision to go to war with Sweden? Was a Russian defeat at Narva entirely predictable? What were the consequences of Russia's defeat?

a) The outbreak of the Great Northern War

In 1699 Peter decided to go to war with Sweden. It was certainly the most fateful decision of his reign, but was it his bravest or his most foolhardy? At the time he saw the need for a new direction in his foreign policy. In January 1699 the Turks signed the Treaty of Karlowitz, ceding extensive territory to Austria, Poland and Venice. The west was now free to concentrate on the question of the Spanish Succession. Russia, which was offered only Azov, refused to sign. Peter attempted to win better terms. But without allies he could apply only limited pressure on the Turks. After long negotiations a 30-year truce was agreed, by which the Russians abandoned none of their claims and received only limited concessions immediately. Russia kept Azov, would pay no more tribute to the Tatars and would have a permanent ambassador in Constantinople on equal terms with the English, French and Austrians. But absolutely no Russian ships, not even merchant vessels, were to be allowed on the Black Sea, and the Turks kept Kerch. After all of the resources he had expended and the military and diplomatic efforts Russia had undertaken, this was a bitter disappointment to Peter. Russia could now advance no farther southward, the only avenue for further expansion lying in the north.

It should perhaps not be surprising that, given the frustrations his efforts in the south were facing, Peter's attention should turn elsewhere. In particular he began to think more about the Swedish possessions on the Baltic, which he had discussed with Augustus. But did an attack on Sweden present a realistic chance of conquests, or was it the only opportunity available – and one fraught with risks? Arguably there were good reasons for going to war. Sweden's possessions included Ingria and Karelia, which had been taken from Russia, and Russia had long wanted them back. (See the map on page 37.) The Swedish army was truly formidable but, with a population of only about 1.5 million, Sweden seemed overstretched in holding this empire together. The new Swedish king, Charles XII, appeared a weak ruler. He had reputedly lived a life as reckless and irresponsible as Peter ever had, hunting bears with a pitchfork because he found using firearms boring. This hardly seemed the lifestyle of a dangerous enemy. Also Russia could find allies. Poland wanted the return of other Swedish conquests, especially Livonia. Denmark resented Swedish possessions on its southern frontier, from which the Swedes could threaten Denmark with a war on two fronts. Finally a Livonian noble, Johann von Patkul, hoping that the Livonian nobility would

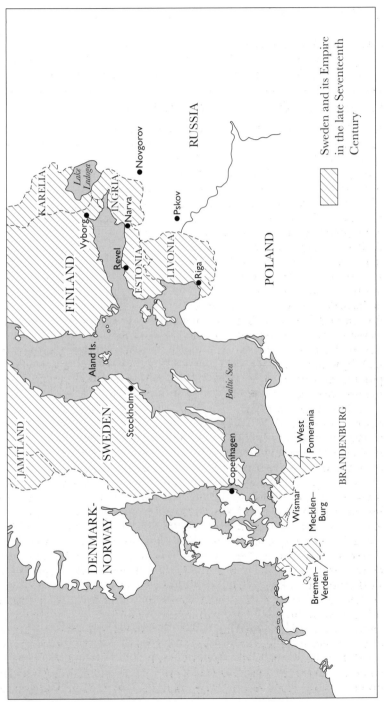

Sweden and its Empire in the late Seventeenth Century.

fare better under Polish rule, worked tirelessly to bring a firm alliance of Sweden's enemies into being.

Patkul's appeals certainly received a sympathetic hearing from Peter. But what were Peter's real motives in joining the anti-Swedish coalition? Klyuchevsky suggested that Patkul 'intended to make Peter, the only serious participant in this comic opera coalition, the dupe of a vulgar farce ... who was to receive the swamps of Ingria and Karelia as a reward for future victories'.[6] Briefly, the Russians would be the alliance's cannon-fodder, and their allies would collect the cream of the spoils. Patkul clearly understood and sought to exploit Peter's ambitions and presented him with a memorandum, which

1 listed all the advantages he would enjoy through possession of a Baltic seaboard, stressing the economic gains; he would be able to trade directly with Holland, England, Spain, Portugal, and in the Mediterranean, as well as to open the trade route from western Europe
5 across Russia to the Far East, from which his profit would be inestimable.[7]

These were factors which would attract Peter. There was also the question of the less than warm reception Peter had received in Swedish-held Riga at the start of the Great Embassy, which the tsar certainly resented deeply. Perhaps also such a war offered Peter the only opportunity for expansion. It was also an area where previous tsars had fought 'long, expensive and eventually unsuccessful struggles against Sweden'.[8] In short, where else could Peter find as much glory as in conquering territory where both Ivan IV and Alexei had tried and failed?

Whatever his motives, he agreed to join an anti-Swedish alliance with Augustus as Elector of Saxony (but not as King of Poland, which remained at peace) and with Frederick IV of Denmark. But he had learnt a modicum of caution and refused to commit himself to attacking Sweden before he had a firm peace with the Turks. In the meantime he sent messages of goodwill and promises of enduring peace to Sweden while he prepared an army. As the peasant levies of his first Azov campaign had been dispersed, and the *streltsy* had been partially disbanded and were completely demoralised after their last mutiny was crushed, the latter was no small task. It was made harder by the resources he had lavished on his fleet at Tagenrog and the fact that the death of Gordon had robbed him of his best military organiser. Still he raised and, after a fashion, trained and equipped 27 new infantry regiments. He was well supplied with artillery – ironically Sweden had supplied him with 300 guns to fight the Turks. But could he have really expected such a scratch force to withstand the Swedish army? Or had he such faith in his allies to believe that a long, hard-fought campaign would be avoided? In either case he was disastrously mistaken.

b) The Battle of Narva

On 9 August 1700, the day after he heard of the truce with the Turks and six months after the Danes and Augustus's Saxon troops had attacked the Swedes, Peter declared war. In doing so he set his foot on a path which would take him to a defeat of staggering proportions at Narva. Was this, in fact, the entirely predictable outcome of haphazardly pitching an ill-prepared force against a ruthless and powerful enemy? The timing of Peter's entry into what was to be called the Great Northern War was certainly deplorable. That very day Denmark capitulated. Peter, his allies, and all Europe were reminded why Sweden was a great power.

The Swedish army was extremely efficient, well trained and well led. But what made it truly formidable was its very clear and aggressive doctrine: the Swedes attacked their enemies and did not trouble overmuch with the niceties of exchanging artillery or musket fire. Instead they had great faith in the efficacy of cold steel. Untried troops – and veterans – regularly collapsed in the face of a savage Swedish charge. Also, contrary to expectations, they had in Charles XII a commander worthy of their abilities. Cold, arrogant and headstrong, the impetuous young king of Sweden rapidly found that his true vocation lay in warfare, and he was determined to defeat all of his enemies completely – no matter how long it took or how much it cost. He also initially had the support of the English and the Dutch, who wanted this war settled quickly: they did not want a long war in the north to distract them from the general European war expected soon over the Spanish Succession. With the support of their warships, Charles had landed an army in Denmark and prepared to attack Copenhagen. With his armies committed in the south, Frederick IV had no choice but to accept Swedish terms and abandon his allies. Hearing the news, Augustus withdrew his Saxon troops from Riga, which they were besieging. Without telling Peter he tried secretly to come to terms with Charles, an early example of the duplicity for which he became famous. He failed to make an agreement since Charles wanted a military victory, not a diplomatic *coup*. But, for the time being, the only enemy available for Charles to attack was the Russian army.

By November 1700 the Russians were besieging Narva, a fortified town blocking Russia's path to the sea. It was a slow business. Autumn rain had reduced the roads to a quagmire, making supplying the Russian force extremely difficult. A sustained artillery bombardment proved impossible. The news that Charles had landed with an army 150 miles away at Pernau, and was marching to relieve the town, caused considerable unease among the Russians. Peter caused a great deal more unease by hurriedly leaving the army on what turned out to be the night before the battle. Even more surprisingly, he took his military commander, Golovin, with him. He left Du Croy in command, an experienced officer but, as an emissary from Augustus, he was not even in Russian service.

Peter's motives caused much speculation. Unsurprisingly, accusations of cowardice have been made. It has been asserted that 'Peter's courage was unequal to the occasion. He displayed his occasional capacity for panic and decided that it was imperative that he be in Moscow as soon as possible'.[9] Others have sought more respectable motives. Robert Massie suggests that Peter had not expected an immediate battle, and had gone to Novgorod to speed up reinforcements and confer with Augustus about his flight from Riga. Whatever his motives, Peter could not have changed his commander at a worse moment. At two p.m. on 20 November Charles attacked amidst a blinding snow storm, with about 10,000 Swedes against 40,000 entrenched Russians. The Swedes smashed through the Russian lines and, with the exception of the Guards regiments, the Russian forces in their path were rapidly reduced to a panic-stricken mob. As hundreds drowned fleeing across the Narva river, some Russian troops began murdering their hated foreign officers, who promptly surrendered to the Swedes. The Russian commanders of thousands of troops who had not yet met the Swedes, and who might easily have counter-attacked and reversed the situation, simply lost heart and tamely capitulated. Fewer than 700 Swedes died compared with well over 8,000 Russian casualties. The entire Russian artillery train was captured and thousands of Russian prisoners were contemptuously sent on their way. Charles had won a brilliant victory.

c) The aftermath of Narva

Perhaps Charles XII's victory was too overwhelming. The Swedish king's already high opinion of his military prowess grew higher still and his already deep contempt for the Russians grew yet more deep. He remained convinced until it was far too late that he could inflict another such humiliation on the Russians whenever he chose. Peter, for his part, was already displaying the resilience he could show in the face of disaster, and he immediately began rebuilding his army. Most historians are highly impressed by the determination, courage and enormous energy he showed in recovering from the defeat. But perhaps we should bear more clearly in mind that he had brought Russia to the brink of utter catastrophe. There was little the Russians could have done to stop a Swedish invasion immediately after Narva. It seems safe to assume that what forces remained to Russia would have met a similar fate to those at Narva if the Swedes had decided to follow up their victory. The Russians were in fact saved from this not by their own efforts but by the decision of Charles. With his troops exhausted and many of them ill after their immense efforts, a winter campaign in Russia, especially against utterly contemptible foes who could be beaten at any time, seemed too much to ask of his army. Instead of pursuing the Russians and knocking them out of the war, Charles decided to turn his back on them and settle with Augustus first.

Perhaps the magnitude of their defeat also prepared the Russian people for a long, hard-fought war, and the great demands that it would impose on them. From the outset these demands were heavy and became heavier with time. If Peter was to buy time for Russia to prepare for its next encounter with Charles, then he had to purchase the expensive, and barely trustworthy, support of Augustus. Obviously the longer Augustus stayed in the field, the longer Charles would have his back turned on Russia. Peter had to pay a price Russia could ill afford. Up to 20,000 Russian troops, munitions, a huge subsidy of 100,000 roubles a year, and the assurance that Augustus would receive the lion's share of the spoils – Livonia and Estonia, while only Ingria would go to Russia – had to be paid to Augustus. Meanwhile Russia had to be mobilised for war to a degree it had never before known. As we shall see (page 85), money had to be raised to pay for imported munitions, entire industries had to be built from scratch, and whole armies had to be raised and properly trained, equipped and armed. New recruits had to be found or conscripted. At least Russia did not face the terrible manpower problems which Sweden was to encounter. The immediate necessity was to replace the artillery. The Russians had to accept the near sacrilege of seeing many of their church bells melted down for gun barrels. Iron founders were threatened with death if they did not produce enough gun carriages. It is generally accepted that out of the ruins of Narva, Peter began to build a modern, westernised – and eventually formidable – Russian army.

Yet it is worth bearing in mind that increased national mobilisation, investment in war industries, and realism in training and equipping his troops were steps which Peter might usefully have made before the battle of Narva! The battle perhaps marked a political coming of age for the tsar, but had it been an excessively long time in arriving? It seems clear that he entered the war naively, with no real idea of what he risked. Like his allies, Peter completely underestimated Charles XII, but surely he should have been aware of the inadequacies of his own army? As matters transpired, Charles had not only provided him with a breathing space he needed to survive, but Sweden's absorption in Poland was to offer glittering opportunities for a tsar with an increasingly capable army. How well Peter was able to exploit these opportunities remains to be seen.

4 Conclusion

KEY ISSUE How best can we sum up Peter's first steps in foreign policy?

Is it possible to perceive between 1695 and 1701 a clear vision in Peter's foreign policy – or was he rushing from project to project, allowing his enthusiasms to blind him to the limits on Russia's strength and ability to pay for them? The quest for a seaport more convenient to European trade and less ice-bound than Archangel can be seen as imperative if Russia was to grow powerful. Russia had also been slowly driving its frontiers south towards the Crimea, and the attack on Azov was perhaps a logical continuation of that drive. When frustrated in his ambitions for a foothold on the Black Sea, an attempt to win a Baltic coastline was also perhaps a sensible move – especially in lands which had once been Russian, and which previous tsars had tried and failed to regain. Indeed a successful aggressive foreign policy must surely contain some degree of opportunism. Forging closer contacts with the west and importing technology and experts was also not a new policy.

Alternatively, we might ask whether a continued advance towards the Black Sea was in any way practical. The Turks were weakened and under pressure from Poland, Austria and Venice, but could Peter really imagine that he could break their grip on the Black Sea and force them to allow ships to pass freely through the Bosphorus to Russian ports? Surely the chances of achieving this must have been seen as extremely remote: even though weakened in Europe, the Turkish grip on the Bosphorus remained secure. If so, for Peter to commit the resources he did to Azov and Tagenrog was a pointless waste. Furthermore, for Peter to spend 18 months outside his country, largely devoted to learning how to build ships, might be described as a task a tsar should properly have delegated. Also for him to join an alliance against a formidable military power like Sweden with only a scratch force to put in the field could easily be seen as absurdly naive.

We could, if we chose, make either a positive or a negative assessment of Peter's foreign policy with equal ease. There is much in it that is equivocal. Perhaps this should caution us against making too hurried, or too sweeping, a judgement. The clarity of Peter's foreign policy aims is indeed a highly debatable issue. There is much in his early foreign policy that appears haphazard and reckless, as Peter leapt from project to project without seeming to weigh the risks or consider Russia's ability to pay the price for success. Perhaps, if we are to see in Narva Peter's political coming of age, we shall see a clearer vision in the tsar's later foreign policy moves. In the next chapter we shall consider whether the defeat at Narva can be seen as a turning point, and whether a new clarity and realism entered Peter's foreign policy.

References

1 Joseph Robertson (ed.), *Pages from the Diary of General Patrick Gordon of Auchleuchries in the Years 1635–1699* (Frank Cass & Co., 1968), p. 184.
2 Cyprian A.G. Bridge (ed.), *History of the Russian Fleet during the Reign of Peter the Great by a Contemporary Englishman* (Navy Records Society, 1899), p. 4.
3 William Bray (ed.), *The Diary of John Evelyn*, vol. 2 (Everyman's Library, 1966), p. 351.
4 Letter by Princess Sophia of Hanover, 11 August 1697, William Marshall, *Peter the Great* (Longman, 1996), p. 98.
5 John Perry, *The State of Russia under the Present Czar* (Frank Cass & Co. Ltd., 1967), p. 166.
6 Vasili Klyuchevsky, *Peter the Great* (Macmillan, 1963), p. 62.
7 Ian Grey, *Peter the Great: Emperor of All Russia* (Hodder & Stoughton, 1962), p. 159.
8 M.S. Anderson, *Peter the Great* (Thames & Hudson, 1978), p. 49.
9 Alex de Jonge, *Fire and Water* (Collins, 1979), p. 150.

Working on chapter 3

Summary Diagram
Peter's early foreign policy

Failures | Achievements

First campaign disastrous ← Azov → Costly victory of second campaign

Failed to find support for claim to Kerch ← Great Embassy → Forged contacts with west and hired technical expertise

Over-ambitious decision for war and utter humiliation of Narva ← Great Northern War → Kept Russia in the war after Narva

Source-based questions on Chapter 3

1. Two views of Peter in the west
Read the extracts by Princess Sophia and Perry on pages 33–4 and answer the following questions:

a) What, in the 1690s, would have made England and the Netherlands so attractive to Peter? (*5 marks*)

b) Why did Sophia make a point of writing that Peter did not get drunk in her presence (line 10)? (*5 marks*)

c) What made Peter such a baffling and fascinating figure to western observers? (*4 marks*)

d) Did the two observers approve or disapprove of Peter's willingness to perform manual labour? (*6 marks*)

Hints and advice: Remember that you have only limited time to answer any question. The ability to budget that time is important. Fortunately the marks allotted to each question give you a very useful guide. Naturally you should not spend most of your time answering a question worth four marks, only to be forced to rush through the rest.

a) Here you are called upon to use your own knowledge of the period. Remember that these two countries were the leading naval powers, and a man with Peter's fascination with the sea would be well aware of it. He must have heard much of them from his associates in the German Quarter. Also remember that they were both at the forefront of technology, of commercial expansion and of science. There was much more to be seen than just ship-building.

b) Remember, when addressing this question, just how little was known of Russia. What the west does know largely came from the accounts of travellers, such as Olearius (see page 13), which were extremely popular either despite or because of the wild exaggerations they contained. How, then, might Sophia have expected Peter to behave?

c) Here you might usefully consider how unusual his *incognito* status was, and what difficulty his presence made for his hosts. Also given his height (six foot seven inches), could he ever realistically have hoped to remain unrecognised? Also, given that Russia was deemed to be a barbarous place, were people waiting for him to act barbarously? If so, did he disappoint them?

d) This is a difficult question. Would these two observers share a common view? Sophia, the western aristocrat, perhaps had fixed ideas concerning men who performed manual labour, and the suitability of a monarch in interesting himself in such things. Perry the engineer would hardly wish to be mistaken for a manual worker himself. But bear in mind that they both saw in Peter an extremely unusual individual, to whom the normal social rules might not apply. Did they, then, both have mixed feelings on this issue? Remember both writers held unspoken assumptions about how a monarch should behave, and your ability to explore these will do much to enhance your marks.

4 The Emergence of a European Power

POINTS TO CONSIDER

How did Russia recover from Narva and become a formidable military power? Did Peter use his new-found strength wisely and to Russia's advantage? In this chapter you will be introduced to the rise of Russia as a European power. Consider where Peter was successful and unsuccessful in his wars and in his diplomacy. Assess how Russia's rise influenced other countries, and indeed how events outside Russia influenced Peter's wars. In short, try to place Russia's rise within the context of European history.

KEY DATES

1702	First Russian victories at Erestfer and Hummelshof.
1703	Russian forces reach the mouth of the river Neva and found St Petersburg.
1704	Russians take Dorpat and Narva.
1706 October 13	Treaty of Altranstadt.
1708	Swedish offensive on Russia begins, battles of Golovchin and Lesnaya.
1709 June 27	Battle of Poltava.
1711	Pruth campaign.
1718 December 11	Death of Charles XII.
1721 August 30	Treaty of Nystadt.

1 Russia's First Victories

> **KEY ISSUE** Which was more important to Russia's recovery from Narva, the policies of Peter or the mistakes of Charles XII?

Arguably, Russia's recovery from the humiliation of Narva was astonishingly rapid. But which was more important to that recovery – the drive and ruthless determination of the tsar or the serious errors of judgement of Charles XII? Turning his back on Russia was one such error. Another was leaving his Baltic provinces poorly defended. To guard against Russian attack he left behind just 7,000 men under major general von Schlippenbach. Probably he expected to defeat Augustus, the Elector of Saxony and Polish King, as rapidly and dramatically as he had dealt with the Danes and the Russians. If so, this was an even greater error. A decisive military victory over Augustus's

Saxon troops proved as elusive as a political settlement which would deprive Augustus of the Polish throne. Augustus was too cunning a politician, and his general, Steinau, too experienced to allow Charles the crushing victory he sought. Charles inflicted a number of defeats on the Saxons, but they always retreated in good order. Politically he was hampered by the fragmentation of Poland, where no effective central authority existed which could be forced to submit to Swedish pressure. Great magnates pursued their own interests, and political alliances were constantly shifting. Charles could control only the parts of Poland his army was currently occupying. Instead of a rapid victory, he was tied down by years of campaigning.

-Profile-

Charles XII, king of Sweden (r. 1697–1718). He ascended the throne at the age of 15. His father had intended that a regency council would rule Sweden until he reached maturity. The regents, however, were eager to ingratiate themselves with their future ruler and involved him in policy-making very quickly. Within months he was declared of age. He had a reputation as a wild and irresponsible youth, but was in fact undergoing a harsh and dangerous regime of physical exercise intended to prepare himself for war. He was very well educated and exceptionally stubborn. Throughout his life he clung obstinately to the severe moral code of his religion and family.

In 1700, with the outbreak of the Great Northern War, he dedicated himself to victory at any price. His early victories over the Saxons and Danes, and over the Russians at Narva, convinced him of his military prowess. He determined to finish with the Saxons before dealing with the Russians. This involved him in several years' campaigning in Poland, giving Peter the time he needed to prepare. Charles invaded Russia in 1708, and the following year his army was destroyed at Poltava. He fled to Turkish territory and remained there until 1714, always hoping to use Turkish power to recover his fortunes. He did design administrative and financial reforms intended to share the cost of the war more fairly between his people, and upon his return he implemented them. This did not, however, offer a solution to the utter exhaustion Sweden was suffering. Determined to prosecute an increasingly hopeless war, he was killed on campaign in Norway in 1718. For all his efforts his reign marked the end of Sweden's great power status.

An obvious and decisive move would have been to attack Saxony itself, which would have broken Augustus's power, as it was his only reliable source of funds and troops. But the west was absorbed by the War of the Spanish Succession, and the English and the Dutch would never tolerate a Swedish army operating in their rear while the issue was undecided. In 1704, at Charles's insistence, Augustus was deposed by a Polish Diet which only wanted to rid itself of foreign armies. Augustus, however, with continuing Russian support, fought on, refusing to accept his deposition. But events in the west freed Charles's hands. With the victories of Blenheim (1704) and Ramillies (1706), the west worried less about his actions. In August 1706 he marched on Saxony. The Saxons were not prepared to see their nation devastated for the sake of their elector's Polish ambitions and offered no resistance. Augustus was left with no option but to accept the Treaty of Altranstadt, agreeing to forfeit the Polish throne and his alliance with Russia. Charles was at last free to settle with Peter.

But had he left it too late? Had the English and the Dutch, in effect, saved Peter? The tsar had unquestionably used his time well. A new Russian army was built, with modern training, modern tactics and strict discipline. [Systematic conscription was introduced, based on a 25-year term of service – which in effect meant life, as few would survive such a period, and those who did would be too old and unfit to be welcomed back in their old villages.] As we shall see (page 93), enormous resources were lavished on this army, and the Russian people had to bear a massive burden of taxation. As early as 1702 this great effort began to pay off, and the Russians began winning victories in the Baltic area. These were modest at first, but as Swedish casualties could not be replaced, Russian successes became increasingly decisive. Sweden's position in its Baltic provinces began to collapse. In July 1702 Sheremetev's victory at Hummelshof destroyed the Swedish field army, leaving Livonia unprotected except for garrisons at Riga, Pernau and Dorpat. The area was ravaged by Cossack and Kalmyk irregular cavalry. Thousands were killed or dragged back to Russia, many to be sold to the Tatars as slaves. Also in 1702 Russian boat squadrons appeared on lake Ladoga and drove Swedish forces away, exposing the key strategic fortress of Nöteborg, which guarded the route down the river Neva to the Baltic. It fell in October 1702, and Peter aptly renamed it Schlüsselburg (Key fortress). Finally, in May 1703, Peter's troops reached the mouth of the Neva. He had won his outlet to the sea (see the map on page 50).

Peter had achieved his war aims, but how could he secure them? He immediately began work on a new harbour, which was to develop into his new capital. But did he do so because he was too impatient to await the capture of an established port, or had he no confidence in his ability to hold one when Charles came east? Perhaps he hoped that Charles could be persuaded to let the Russians retain a port they had constructed themselves, in an area in which the Swedes had never

Peter the Great's Baltic Conquests.

shown any interest. If so, he still did not appreciate the obstinacy of the Swedish king and still feared his military power. But as we shall see (page 66), while Charles stayed away St Petersburg grew unhindered. The Swedish navy 'never made a bold attack, deterred with the appearance of a fortification ... that could bring few guns to bear'.[1] Their only attempted landing was a shambles, the Swedes showing astonishing incompetence for a naval power. Russian conquests spread along the Baltic coast, through Ingria, Estonia, Livonia and into Courland. Peter built a new Baltic fleet, several ships of which were constructed well enough to 'vie with the best in Europe'.[2] But had he any idea how to end the war? He had been making increasingly frantic attempts to make peace. He approached the English, the Prussians, the Danes and even the French to mediate a settlement, willing to send troops to either side in their war. But nobody would assist Russia, and Charles was not interested. Despite Peter's victories the Swedish troops still boasted that they could 'drive the Russian rabble not only out of their own country, but even out of the world, with no other weapons but their whips'.[3] In August 1707 they began their march east to prove it.

2 The Swedish Invasion

> **KEY ISSUE** Given the size and population of Russia, was a
> Swedish invasion doomed before it began?

Where do the roots of Sweden's catastrophe at Poltava lie – in the strength of the new Russian army and Peter's ruthless strategy, or in the arrogance and continuing errors of judgement of Charles? Estimates of the numbers involved in the campaign vary, but it appears that Charles commanded about 33,000 troops, with over 11,000 at Riga under Lowenhaupt who were to join him with a great supply train, and 14,000 in Finland under Lybecker to attack St Petersburg (they in fact achieved nothing). Peter had about 135,000 troops. Given such a disparity of forces, should Peter be credited with a victory due to his 'long-term strategy which had helped manoeuvre Charles into a position in which he could not win'?[4] Alternatively, should we conclude that Charles was doomed from the start to suffer the same fate as later, more powerful, invaders of Russia (Napoleon and Hitler)? Peter's scorched earth policy – devastating vast swathes of land through which the Swedes might march – was certainly as effective as it was ruthless. Even the recently conquered town of Dorpat was razed to the ground to deny the Swedes supplies. This indeed robbed the Swedish offensive of its momentum and forced Charles to halt at Mogilev from July to September 1708 to await Lowenhaupt's supplies (see map on page 50).

The Swedish invasion of Russia.

But was this devestation necessary? The Russian army was fighting well. At the battle of Golovchin (4 July 1708) the Russians had fought stubbornly and retreated in good order – a creditable achievement against such a formidable foe. Admitedly the stakes were high, but would Peter not have served Russia better by risking an early, decisive battle, rather than devastating his own country? Was he being overly timid of the Swedish army, or entirely realistic of Russian chances against the Swedes before they had been weakened? Perhaps, inadvertently, his delaying tactics were more effective in giving Charles the chance to make major mistakes than they were in weakening the enemy. For Charles certainly made disastrous errors. Firstly Lowenhaupt was very late, and Charles finally lost patience and decided to march south to Severia to find the supplies he needed. This movement exposed Lowenhaupt's force, which was in fact only days away, to a Russian attack. At the resulting battle of Lesnaya (28 September 1708) Lowenhaupt managed to extricate about half of his force but had to destroy his desperately needed supplies. Furthermore by the time Charles reached Severia, the Russians had devastated that province also. The Swedes had to continue south – they assumed that their assault on Moscow was delayed, in fact it was cancelled.

Charles XII's best hope now was to take advantage of the seething discontent that Peter's exactions had raised in Russia. There had been recent uprisings by the Bashkirs, the Don Cossacks and in Astrakhan, but as we shall see (page 104) these were treated ruthlessly. However, potential allies existed. Mazeppa, *hetman* (elected leader) of the Ukrainian Cossacks, gambling on being on the winning side, threw in his lot with Charles after 21 years of loyalty to Peter. Yet before the Swedes could reach his capital of Baturin, Peter's favourite, Menshikov, had destroyed the town and the stores the Swedes needed so desperately, also massacring the population. Cowed, only a handful of Ukrainian Cossacks supported Mazeppa. When the Zaporozhsky Cossacks showed similar Swedish sympathies, their capital, the Sech, received the same treatment. The Tatars wanted to support Charles, but Peter refitted enough warships at Tagenrog to make their Turkish overlords hesitate in permitting them to do so. Consequently the Swedes suffered a terrible winter at Romny, where bitter cold, isolation and lack of supplies caused dreadful suffering. In the spring Charles made his last mistake of the campaign by refusing to abandon it even then. Instead he ordered a siege of Poltava, an important strategic point whose capture would allow the Swedes to re-open contact with Poland. By the time Peter was willing to risk a major battle to save the town, the Swedish army was as weakened as he could have hoped. At the battle of Poltava (28 June 1709), Charles, still utterly confident of a quick victory but too ill from a wound to command personally, ordered 19,000 of his troops to launch one of the famed Swedish attacks upon 42,000 well

Peter I at Poltava by J.G. Dannhauer, 1710s.

entrenched Russians. A few hours later his army was shattered, and with it was shattered Sweden's status as a great power. Nearly 7,000 Swedes were dead, nearly 3,000 taken prisoner. Russian dead numbered just 1,345. A few days later (1 July), at Perevoluchna, most of the remnants, over 14,000 troops, surrendered also. Charles, with just a handful of followers, was in flight to the sanctuary of Turkish territory. (See the map on page 50.)

3 The Pruth Campaign

> **KEY ISSUES** Why did Peter repeat every mistake which led Charles XII to disaster at Poltava, and why did he escape so lightly?

Peter had won a great victory, and the fruits of victory arrived quickly. Suddenly Russia was a power worth courting, and European monarchs began to ponder the advantages of dynastic alliances with the Romanovs. Peter was able to marry his son, Alexis, to Charlotte, daughter of the duke of Wolfenbüttel, and his niece, Anne, to the duke of Courland. These were relatively minor German states, but the alliances still mark a major shift in Russia's international standing. A new anti-Swedish alliance was formed. Also Sweden was too weak to prevent further Russian advances into its Baltic provinces. In the summer of 1710, with help from its new fleet, Russia captured both Viborg and Riga, securing a wide stretch of the Baltic coast around St Petersburg. The original alliance had agreed that Livonia and Riga would be the prizes of Poland. Now Peter decided to keep them. The fruits of victory were truly sweet. Indeed Dannhauer's portrait of Peter as a conquering warrior king (see page 52) gave an image of himself he had long coveted. But had Peter – like Charles at Narva – won too great a victory? What else can explain the towering over-confidence which led him to repeat the Swede's worst mistakes, bringing him close to utter disaster, in an avoidable war with the Turks?

For Peter, there was only one inconvenient drawback to his new international position: he was still at war, and Charles XII still was not ready to accept defeat. Charles, furthermore, hoped to recover his fortunes with Turkish help. Growing Russian military might was causing anxiety to the Turks, many of whom now regretted not intervening when the Swedish army was in the field. Charles began to rouse the Turks to war. Perhaps over-confident after Poltava, the Russians played into his hands with their uncompromising line with Constantinople. Their demand that Charles be expelled from their territory encouraged the Turks to declare war on 21 November 1710. The result was the Pruth campaign, when Peter led 54,000 troops into Turkish territory. He was assured by

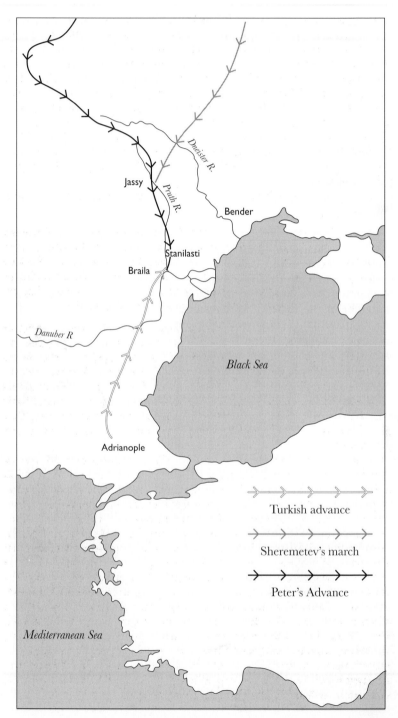

Danuber R

Dniester R.

Jassy

Pruth R.

Bender

Stanilasti

Braila

Black Sea

Adrianople

Mediterranean Sea

Turkish advance

Sheremetev's march

Peter's Advance

The Pruth Campaign.

the *hospodars* (princes) of Walachia and Moldovia that he would be greeted as a liberator, and could raise another 40,000 troops when he arrived – a small enough force in total to face 200,000 Turks. The support and supplies he expected did not, however, materialise in any significant quantity. Peter soon found himself in the position of Charles at Poltava – deep in enemy territory, isolated from support, short of supplies and facing an enemy massed in overwhelming numbers. After a brief but bloody fight the Russians found themselves surrounded at Stanilasti (9 July 1711). Unlike Charles at Poltava, there was no way for Peter to escape even without his army. He was totally at the mercy of the Turks. (See the map on page 54.)

How had he put himself in such a position? Robert Massie held that he had:

1   adopted Charles' role and plunged impetuously into the Ottoman Empire, trusting for support and provisions from an ally who proved unfaithful. He had been misinformed about the strength of the Turkish army, and he had miscalculated the speed with which the Grand Vizier
5   could move. He had continued his advance even after learning that the Turkish army was across the Danube and marching north.[5]

Clearly Peter had made a number of errors, though ranking them in importance is a matter for some debate. The immediate question he had to face was how to extricate himself from this position. The Turks had no need to negotiate: they could easily force the Russians to surrender unconditionally or massacre them. To buy peace Peter faced paying a terrible price in territory, possibly including the loss of Azov and parts of the Ukraine. Perhaps the Turks would also demand that he make peace with Sweden and surrender all of his northern conquests.

Peter was in fact saved by the Turkish grand vizier, Mehemet Baltadji, who wanted a quick end to the war. Russian cavalry (which Peter had earlier detached) were operating in his rear destroying his supplies. His elite troops, the *janissaries*, had suffered heavy losses, and were sullen at the prospect of further fighting – and a grand vizier who angered the *janissaries* could easily meet a sudden, violent death. Also he feared Austrian intervention while he was committed against the Russians. Thus Peter escaped astonishingly lightly, having to return Azov and Tagenrog, abandon his fleet there and remove his ambassador from Constantinople. Baltadji ignored Swedish interests and only demanded that the Russians evacuate their forces from Poland and allow Charles passage home. After returning to Russia, Peter showed no enthusiasm for implementing even these mild terms, and the Turks declared war three more times – though no campaigns were fought – before a final settlement was reached. The clauses concerning Poland were never properly enforced, and Charles wisely did not rely on a Russian promise of a safe passage.

4 The New Anti-Swedish Alliance

> **KEY ISSUE** Did Peter undermine his new-found international prestige through inept diplomacy?

Though humiliated on the Pruth, Peter survived with his strength intact, and Russia's new-found standing in Europe was not seriously affected. The new anti-Swedish coalition that had been forming continued to develop. Sweden's defeat at Poltava encouraged Denmark to re-enter the war and invade southern Sweden. Augustus repudiated the Treaty of Altranstadt and reclaimed the Polish throne. New allies appeared, eager to share in the spoils of Sweden's defeat. Frederick I of Prussia was one such ally, even if he had no intention of actually participating in the fighting if he could avoid it. Another was George Louis, Elector of Hanover, and soon to be king George I of Britain, who wanted the Swedish provinces of Bremen and Verden. Yet even though he was far away, with his army destroyed, his kingdom exhausted by the war, and facing an even more powerful alliance than ever before, Charles XII *still* would not consider coming to terms with his enemies. But if Sweden was so exhausted, its military might desperately weakened by its disastrous invasion of Russia, and its enemies stronger than ever, how was it possible for the war to continue 12 years after Poltava? One possible explanation is that while Peter had secured his war aims before Poltava, his allies were more eager to secure the Swedish provinces they coveted than they were to end the war. It certainly seems clear that there was little holding this alliance together beyond avarice. It is also clear that the allies did not work well together, and indeed the anti-Swedish alliance was transformed into an anti-Russian alliance. Was this the unavoidable result of Russia's rise to become the dominating power in the Baltic? Could the Russians have done nothing to prevent foreign jealousy and suspicion of their new-found power turning into hostility? Or should we say that it was Peter's inept and clumsy diplomacy which left him isolated?

The growth of Russia as a Baltic power was obvious and rapid. Never one to employ half-measures when it came to his navy, Peter lavished vast resources on his new Baltic fleet. The lack of a merchant marine and a relatively small coastline for it to defend, however, left foreign powers uneasy about his motives. They suspected that he intended to take complete control of all Baltic trade. This would be a serious matter, since maritime nations such as England depended on the pitch and timber of the Baltic to keep their fleets in service. Russian control of this trade would be a threat impossible for foreign powers to ignore. But Peter himself ignored such concerns and built, captured or purchased 71 warships for the Baltic. Not that he ever had a fleet of such a size in service. By 1724 one ship had been captured by the Swedes, 20 broken up, 11 were too old and unfit for service, 10 were sunk or run aground and 12 were unfit for heavy seas or described as 'old and crazy'. One English contemporary felt that the fleet's greatest weakness was in its officers, few of whom shared Peter's enthusiasm for the sea. As a result, despite Peter's naval ambitions, the fleet had 'never been in any action worth taking notice of, and always four to one, when ought of that kind offered'.[6] Russia's most effective weaponry in the Baltic, in fact, was not the great ships-of-the-line which Peter loved, but the much smaller and cheaper galleys. Peter used over 200 galleys and large boats, which could operate too close inshore for Swedish ships-of-the-line to engage, to launch brutal raids on the Swedish and Finnish coasts from 1713. Against such raids the Swedes were largely defenceless. Peter's galleys even won a significant victory over larger Swedish ships at the battle of Hangö (6 August 1714), when the wind dropped on a Swedish squadron sailing too close to the shore, and its vessels were promptly overwhelmed by Russian infantry boarding from the galleys. They captured one ship-of-the-line, a frigate and nine small ships, giving Russia its first real naval victory ever. As a result Swedish ships were driven from the upper Baltic, and foreign concerns heightened even more.

But no matter how damaging these raids were, the war dragged on. Swedish resolve was stiffened when, after five years in Turkish territory, Charles XII made a dramatic dash across Europe to reach the Swedish-held city of Stralsund in northern Germany (10 November 1714). Here he resolved to remain, and withstood a siege by Saxon, Danish and Prussian troops until December 1715. He then returned to Sweden, as determined to fight on as ever. Indeed in February 1716 he led an army into Norway. How then was Peter, with his flimsy coalition, to end the war? An invasion of Sweden was an obvious solution. This would be a major undertaking, and it would require dependable allies. But Peter's growing sea power and his apparently insatiable territorial appetite were already antagonising his partners. Why then, in these circumstances, did he choose to intervene in German affairs? Did he see the need to strengthen Russia's position in central Europe, or was the temptation to exercise his new-found international standing, for the sake of exercising it, simply too great? He certainly alarmed his partners in April 1716 by marrying his niece, Catherine, to the duke of Mecklenberg, who was supplied with a Russian garrison.

Peter seemed to be aiming to dominate northern Germany, which Hanover and Prussia could never tolerate. He also provoked a major crisis in the coalition in September 1716, when, after the coalition spent months preparing to invade Sweden, he unilaterally cancelled the operation four days before it was due to start. Are we to believe his explanations – that it was too late in the year to begin such an invasion, and that the Swedes would copy his own scorched earth policy, leaving the invaders without supplies and risking utter disaster? Or should we perhaps suspect that he did not trust his partners to support his army after it had been committed? Whatever his reasons, his decision left 29,000 Russian troops in Denmark, and he was suspected of having planned from the start to gather them there on the pretext of the intended invasion, really meaning to use them to occupy and rule northern Germany. Bernstorff, the chief minister of Hanover, was so alarmed that he tried to get the tsar seized and held hostage until Russian forces returned home.

Perhaps it was because he recognised the serious tensions between Russia and its partners, and thought that Russia urgently needed the protection of some form of international alliance, that in the spring of 1717 Peter visited France. He proposed that Russia replace Sweden as France's ally in the east. Yet he was ignoring the fact that France was recovering from a ruinous war and that its regent, the duc d'Orleans, was pursuing a policy of friendship with Britain. Such an alliance would in fact infuriate the British and give France little in return. Once again, Peter was disappointed. Despite, or perhaps because of his efforts, Russia was becoming dangerously isolated. This gave Charles and his new minister, von Goertz, a chance to break up the coalition against Sweden. Von Goertz began negotiating with the coalition members separately, tempting them with the idea of joining Sweden in an attack on their partners. In 1718 he offered peace to Russia, in return for which Russia would return some territory and join an attack on Hanover. These were terms which Peter was certainly willing to consider. But Russia's isolation offered much greater opportunities for Sweden to recover its fortunes. Besides, Charles would never have agreed to the smallest territorial demands Peter would have accepted. Hanover was also showing much greater interest in joining an anti-Russian alliance with Sweden.

Nothing was concluded before Charles was killed on campaign in Norway (11 December 1718). His sister, Ulrika Eleonora, seized the throne (she soon stepped aside for her husband, Frederick) and executed the unpopular von Goertz. But von Goertz had still won a diplomatic victory: he had isolated Russia, and persuaded the Elector of Hanover (now also king of Britain) to join with Sweden to limit Russian gains. In July 1719 a British fleet entered the Baltic with orders to force Russia to make peace on terms favourable to Hanover. But how vulnerable was Russia to British diplomatic and naval pressure? Peter had no merchant shipping for the British to threaten, and his fleet did not venture out to challenge the British. How then were the British to force terms upon the tsar? Only a major attack on the Russian coast or a threat to St Petersburg might have moved Peter. But this would require a full-scale military commitment. Peter was allowing trade with Britain to continue unhampered, and there was little British interest in their king's Hanoverian ambitions. As well as being unable to harm Russia, the British fleet also found that it could not protect Sweden. The light-drafted Russian galleys continued to devastate the Swedish coast, operating too close to the shore for the British ships-of-the-line to stop them.

The anti-Russian coalition was frustrated, and with it was frustrated Sweden's last hope of saving part of its empire. On 10 September 1721 Frederick accepted that the war was lost, and the Treaty of Nystadt was signed. This gave Russia all of Livonia, Estonia, Ingria and Karelia as far as Vyborg. In return Sweden received little: the return of Finland and of Swedish prisoners, a payment of 2 million *thalers*, the right to buy Livonian grain duty free, and a promise that Russia would not interfere in Sweden's internal affairs.

5 The War with Persia

> **KEY ISSUE** After an exhausting two decades of war, why did Peter embark almost immediately upon a new military adventure?

Russia celebrated an end to 21 years of war with an immense sense of relief. As we shall see, the war had led Peter to impose terrible burdens on his people, who were in a number of cases driven to revolt. Over 300,000 men had been conscripted, of whom perhaps one-third had died, been disabled or deserted. Civilian deaths due to his scorched earth policy and the exactions he made to fight his war are unknown, but must have been heavy. The tax burden on Russia had risen from about 1.5 million roubles in 1680 to 8.7 million in 1724. Nearly all of this was spent on war. As we shall also see (page 70), a stunning amount of state revenues were embezzled by officials and thus the real cost of the war to the Russian people must have been terrible indeed. What Russia desperately needed was a period of peace and recovery. Why then, while the celebrations were still in progress, was Peter preparing for a new war? Had opportunities arisen that could not be ignored? Or was Peter, after lavishing so much time, effort and resources on his military might, unwilling to see it stand idle? Had he simply devoted so much of his life to warfare that it seemed the natural state of affairs? Even before the end of the Great Northern War, his attention was being drawn in other directions. In 1716, hearing reports of gold in central Asia, he sent an expedition to the khanates of Khiva and Bukhara. Unfortunately this expedition was massacred due to the incompetence of its leader. In 1719 he sent an ambassador to negotiate an increase of trade with the Chinese, but his approaches were rebuffed. He had greater success in the north-east, annexing the Kamchatka Peninsula (see the map at the beginning of this book on page viii); and, in 1724, he ordered Bering to undertake his first expedition to find if Russia and America were separated by the sea. He also showed a keen interest in establishing trade with India and ordered a naval expedition there, which, due to poorly prepared ships and unenthusiastic leadership, never left the Baltic.

In short, Peter found little immediate return for his initiatives away from the Baltic. Did he dream of conquering territories even greater in scope than anything his predecessors had achieved – especially Ivan IV, who conquered the khanates of Astrakhan and Kazan? He certainly toyed with thoughts of the great wealth Russia might win if it could divert the silk trade through St Petersburg, away from its traditional route via the Mediterranean. Perhaps this explains why he was not able to resist taking advantage of the collapsing power of the Persian Safavid dynasty. Also the weakness of the dynasty might lead to intervention from Persia's traditional enemy: the Ottoman empire. An extension of Turkish power along more of Russia's southern frontier was not a threat to be taken lightly.

Whatever Peter's motives, the murder of Russian traders in Persia by bandits provided him with an excuse to intervene. He claimed that he was acting to protect Russian trade and assist the shah to restore order. But he really intended to seize Persia's Caucasian provinces. In July 1722, 61,000 regular and irregular troops and sailors set out from Astrakhan (see the map on page 61). This was a very large force considering the feebleness of his opponent. But after his experiences during the Pruth campaign he refused to appeal to Christians to rise, and would not depend on any aid that they might offer. He intended to take the strategic and commercial city of Derbent and continue south through Baku and establish a Russian military and commercial base at the mouth of the river Kura. Only then would he conclude a treaty with the Georgian and Armenian Christians.

Superficially the campaign was successful. Baku was taken in July 1723. Soon the Russians had secured three of Persia's provinces on the Caspian coast. But the cost was extremely high. The troops suffered dreadfully in the climate. Far more perished from the heat than from the fighting. Financially the cost was also enormous – at the very least a million roubles. Even more crucially, Peter had blithely overlooked the fact that the Turks would no more allow the Russians a free hand in the Caucasus than he would allow them a free hand there. In particular the Turks would never allow Russia to take territory on the Black sea coast. They threatened war if the Russians moved into Georgia and Armenia. But instead of fighting over the territory, the two powers partitioned it. If Peter dreamed of marching through Persia and Afghanistan to India he was frustrated; all he won was a strip of land along the coast of the Caspian Sea.

In 1732 Anne abandoned the Caucasian provinces – they were too expensive to occupy. But under Catherine the Great the Russians returned, this time to stay. Should, then, Peter's last campaign be written off as a massively expensive folly, or should we see a clear vision of Russia's interests – a campaign fought perhaps before its time? Perhaps in answering this question, we might consider the long-term

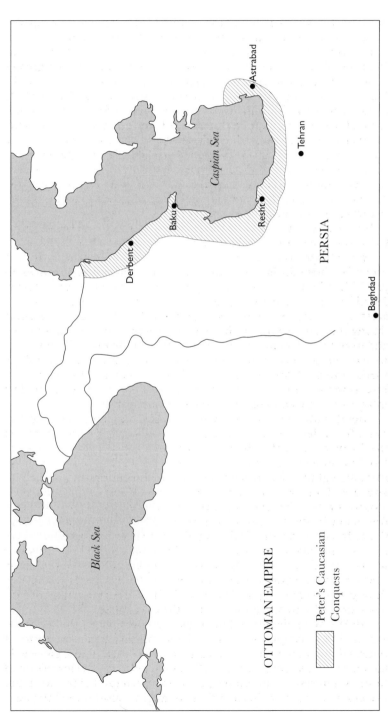

Peter's Caucasian Conquests.

effects of Peter's southern policy suggested by Alexandre Bennigsen: that the Turks 'understood that only a strong religious cohesion, based on the iron discipline of a *Sufi* brotherhood, could check the Russian advance in the future'.[7] In short Peter's failure to rapidly conquer the territory allowed the Turks time to disseminate a militant and mystical branch of Islam in the Caucasus. This was to cause the Russians enormous problems when they finally did conquer the area, problems, especially in Chechnya, which still trouble Russian rulers today.

6 Conclusion

> **KEY ISSUE** What did Russia achieve from all of Peter's wars?

The Persian campaign was the last which Peter fought. He returned to St. Petersburg to give Russia its first full year of peace since Sophia's regency, before his death in 1725. How, then, shall we evaluate his foreign policy? Tsar Alexei had conquered more land, and more valuable land, from Poland with less stress on Russia. But the significance of Peter's conquests lay not in the value of the land, but in the strategic value of the outlet to the Baltic. Also two long-standing enemies of Russia – an already weakened Poland and a still formidable Sweden – had been broken as threats to Russia. Under Peter, furthermore, Russia had become a power to be reckoned with in Europe – a factor which could no longer be ignored by European statesmen. But at what cost? We shall be looking at the resistance to Peter's rule (see page 100) and at the terrible burden of his exactions and the general upheaval Russia endured during his reign at a later point. But it should already be clear that the Russian nation as a whole, alongside significant allies, had to produce a monumental effort in order to defeat Sweden – a power of definitely limited resources and population. Furthermore, was Peter aiming to meet the long-term needs of Russia in his wars for outlets to the sea, or was he only aiming to satisfy his own naval ambitions? We might also ask whether he could have ended the war earlier, or did Charles XII's stubbornness make this impossible? How much of Russia's resources were wasted or mis-directed in pursuit of impossible goals along the Pruth or in Persia? There is no simple answer to these questions. Questions of success and failure in foreign policy, as in so much else, depend upon the perspective of the observer. Such questions also depend upon our assessment of Peter's motives. Was even he clear about his aims beyond his dream of making Russia a great power? Yet these are questions which we, as historians, must address.

References

1 Cyprian A.G. Bridge (ed.), *History of the Russian Fleet during the Reign of Peter the Great by a Contemporary Englishman (1724)* (Navy Records Society, 1899), p. 12.
2 Bridge, *History of the Russian Fleet*, p. 11.
3 Friedrich Christian Weber, *The Present State of Russia*, vol. II, (1722–23) (Frank Cass, 1968), p. 297.
4 Alex de Jonge, *Fire and Water: a Life of Peter the Great* (Collins, 1979), p. 174.
5 Robert K. Massie, *Peter the Great: His Life and World* (Gollancz, 1981), p. 564.
6 Bridge, *History of the Russian Fleet*, p. 116.
7 Alexandre Bennigsen, 'Peter the Great, the Ottoman empire, and the Caucasus', *Canadian-American Slavic Studies*, vol. 8, no. 2, 1974, p. 317.

Working on chapter 4

Summary Diagram
The fruits of victory

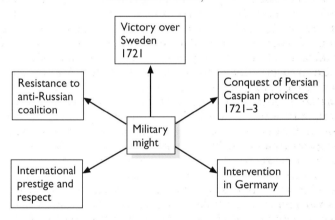

Answering structured and essay questions on Chapter 4

Structured questions on Peter's foreign policy may deal with specific events or be more sweeping in their scope.

1. **a)** Why did Charles XII delay his assault on Russia until 1708?
  b) What were the main causes of the Swedish defeat at the battle of Poltava?
  c) How well did Peter exploit his victory in his dealings with other nations?
2. **a)** In what ways did Russia become a more formidable military power during the Great Northern War?
  b) What did Russia gain from its victory?

Hints and advice: Some examining boards may specify how many marks each section of these questions is worth. If so, you have an obvious guide to how much time to devote to each section. If they do not, you must use your common sense. A question which is descriptive will certainly carry fewer marks than one inviting analysis.

In question 1 the three sections are very specific. In section a) you are invited to describe the factors which delayed Charles XII in Poland. Remember the significance of events in the west. You might also consider his opinions of Russians, and his belief in himself. Section b) invites a brief summary of important factors. This is a simple task, but it contains very real pitfalls. You are asked to describe the main factors, not to scribble down everything you can remember. You must show your examiner not only that you know what the factors are, but also that you can discriminate between events of primary importance and those of secondary importance. Section c) requires a more analytical approach, you must evaluate the relative importance of the benefits Peter won (leadership of a new coalition etc.), with his failures (the suspicion with which his new-found strength was viewed, the fact that he could not end the war, etc.)

In question 2 you need to show a wider awareness of the period. Again, remember that your discussion must be both relevant and discriminatory. Remember when addressing section b) you are not being invited simply to describe the terms of the Treaty of Nystadt, though you must certainly show that you know them; you must also discuss their significance. Did Russia gain anything more than territory, and, if so, what? Did Peter succeed in making Russia a great power?

Essay questions dealing with Peter's foreign policy sometimes address Russia and the west, sometimes they deal with his entire career.

1 How successful was Peter the Great in making Russia part of the European international system?

2 'In foreign affairs he was more successful as a soldier than as a diplomat.' How far do you agree with this verdict of Peter the Great?

An acceptable essay will have an introduction, a main body and a conclusion. In your introductory paragraph you should explain the meaning of the question, raise the issues to be addressed in answering the question, each being worth at least a paragraph in discussion, and briefly outline your argument. Better answers will discuss a number of arguments from your reading, their strengths and weaknesses being discussed in the body of your essay. Take pains on this introduction: if written successfully it will set you in the right direction, allow you to engage with the question and avoid irrelevancies, and, above all, help you avoid the cardinal sin of writing narrative instead of analysis. Your examiners will be looking for a balanced, sustained argument throughout your answer, and anything less will cost you marks.

Question 1 obviously is about the relationship between Russia and the west. Therefore Peter's involvement with such as the Crimean Tatars and with Persia need not be brought in unless you can show a direct relevance. Equally obviously, the Great Northern War and the rise of Russian military might are central to this discussion. But what else should be included? Should you examine the Great Embassy simply because it involved Peter and the west? You must draw up a list of the factors worth surveying, such as Peter's naval power in the Baltic, his perhaps inept diplomacy, etc. What will your central argument be? Was Russia part of the European international system by Peter's death, or was it still on the periphery of Europe, of immediate concern only to its neighbours?

In question 2 you are dealing with Peter's entire career. Remember you are being asked to assess the relative significance of two elements of his foreign policy – diplomacy and war. Consider where Peter had success in war, and also failure. Also consider where he had both success and failure in his diplomacy. Can you find instances where Peter gained his ends without having to resort to force, or will you argue that it was only his military victories that made any diplomacy on his part of interest to the outside world? Bear in mind that you do not have to limit your attentions to the west, but the west will probably take up the bulk of your essay.

5 Transforming the Government

POINTS TO CONSIDER

This chapter will discuss the major reforms instituted by Peter in the machinery of government The central issues to consider are how radical these reforms were: was a more modern, efficient and centralised system of government introduced? Was Peter's rule absolute? Were these changes superficial, leaving a hopelessly corrupt and chaotic system in place?

KEY DATES

1699 *Ratusha* instituted.
1708 *Gubernii* established.
1711 Senate founded.
1718 Foundation of the Colleges.
1721 Holy Synod established.

Peter's reign was dominated by his wars. They also dominated his domestic policies. Peter placed unprecedented burdens on Russia in pursuit of military victories, and soon found that Russia's system of government was not adequate to meet the demands placed upon it. He had to face the urgent task of making his administration more efficient: that is, of course, more efficient in extracting from his people the money and services he needed. But, we must ask, did he in the process have a more profound impact upon the way Russia was ruled?

1 St Petersburg

> **KEY ISSUE** Why did Peter go to such efforts to found a new city on a site never before seen as suitable for settlement?

Peter's most obvious innovation for Russia's government was to supply the nation with a new capital. Reaching the mouth of the river Neva in May 1703, he chose not to wait until he had seized a seaport from Sweden, which he might never be able to hold, but to establish a new Baltic port at that spot. It was hardly an auspicious location. It had never been seen as a suitable location for a port by those who had sailed the Baltic. It was a broad, flat, empty marshland. Strong winds from the south west could submerge the islands upon which Peter

The Admiralty, St Petersburg.

chose to build. It was also a bitterly cold place, and the Neva was usually icebound for over half of the year. (Neva was, in fact, the Finnish word for swamp!) Undeterred, Peter had made up his mind, and he doggedly clung to his new city (named after his name saint), despite eventually winning fully established ports, such as Narva and Reval from Sweden. He lavished on it the attention and resources he rarely showed for anything but his military. On 16 May 1703 the first digging began. For the unfortunate peasants conscripted for the building work, conditions were terrible. No adequate provisions were made for the workforce. The brutally hard working conditions, along with scurvy, dysentery and malaria, killed possibly 25,000, possibly many more.

Peter was delighted when in November 1703 the first ship docked, generously rewarding its Dutch captain. He set his tolls at under half of the Swedish level. He also took steps to divert trade from Archangel, which had previously been Russia's only point of contact with the west, with dire consequences for that port. But he wanted more than just a successful port: he wanted a great city, a rival to those he had seen in the west. He engaged the architect Domenico Trezzini, who gave the city its ornate and ostentatious northern baroque style (see page 67). In order to coerce Russia into supplying the materials and craftsmen he needed, he forbade any stone building elsewhere in Russia. He also used force to people his new city. This included ordering his own family to live there. Nobles, merchants and artisans were required to move there, and build houses at their own expense. They were given no choice about the location or design of their new dwellings. Peter wanted a planned and orderly city and these questions were decided for them. The low-lying islands were often flooded. The barren countryside could not feed the city, and the prices of food and other basics were exorbitant.

Called the Babylon of the Snows, and the Venice of the North, early St Petersburg was a cold, damp, dismal location. In winter it saw only three or four hours' daylight. Determined to make Russians a maritime people, Peter ordered that the inhabitants sail, not row, boats from island to island. Even so, virtually none loved the sea as he did. Unsurprisingly many longed to return to the comforts of Moscow. John Perry wrote how:

> among some other causes, one of the chief which makes the generality
> of the nobility at present uneasy, is, that the Czar obliges them against
> their will to live at Petersburgh, with their wives and families, where
> they are obliged to build new houses for themselves, and where all
> 5 manner of provisions are usually three or four times as dear ... [as] at
> Mosco; which happens from the great expense of it at Petersburgh, and
> the small quantity which the country hereabouts produces, being more
> than two-thirds woods and bogs. ... Whereas in Mosco, all the lords
> and men of distinction, have not only very large buildings within the city,

10 but also their country seats and villages, where they have their fish-
ponds, their gardens, with plenty of several sorts of fruit ... but
Petersburgh ... is too cold to produce these things. Besides, Mosco is
the native place which the Russes are fond of, and where they have
their friends and acquaintances about them; their villages are near, and
15 their provision comes easy and cheap to them.[1]

Red Square, Moscow, 1801.

Yet by 1725 the city had 40,000 inhabitants. Indeed it had by 1712
become the capital of Russia. There was no decree making it so, but
gradually the administration moved there. To most of those forced to
live there it was an expensive, cold and miserable place of exile. To
Peter it was his 'Eden and Paradise', even when his own house was
knee-deep and more in floodwater. Perhaps, as Lindsey Hughes suggests, he was well aware of the city's drawbacks and was using the
terms ironically. But what is clear is that he was prepared to commit
whatever resources it took to establish his new city, and that there was
little in Russia that he would not have sacrificed before he sacrificed
St Petersburg. This was indeed Russia's 'window onto the west'. Was
Russia turning to the west in other ways? Was Peter's new capital sym-
bolic of a transformation of Russia, or merely the most obvious
element of a very superficial change?

2 Central Government Reforms

> **KEY ISSUE** What was Peter's main aim in his government
> reforms?

One of Peter's main claims to greatness rests on his transformation of
Russia's system of government – that he established new institutions
which were not only more modern and efficient but which represented a centralisation of Russia's administration, making Russia in
effect an absolutist state. But did these reforms amount to a fundamental transformation of the state, or were they merely superficial
changes to an irreparably corrupt and inefficient system?

The system of government Peter inherited was essentially medieval.
It was based on *prikazy* (government departments or chancelleries)
which had evolved in an extremely haphazard and confusing manner.
Some *prikazy* were established to deal with immediate problems, then
dissolved. Some dealt with specific administrative functions – the
Pomestnyi prikaz, for instance, dealt with the lands and peasants owned
by the nobility. Others exercised a great many administrative functions over specific territories, such as the *Sibirskii prikaz*, which administered Siberia. There was, furthermore, no clear demarcation of
duties. Especially in the fields of raising revenue and administering
justice, their responsibilities frequently overlapped. Previous tsars had
further confused the matter by assigning new tasks to existing *prikazy*
seemingly at random. Alexei established the *Tainyi* (Secret) *prikaz*
initially to supervise his falconers, but eventually it became responsible for his diplomatic correspondence, the fishing and salt industries and the business of one of his favourite monasteries! By Peter's
reign it was often impossible to be sure which *prikaz* was responsible
for which duty. Even more importantly for Peter, the collection of
revenue was divided between so many *prikazy* that the tsar could have
little idea how much money the state received, still less how much it
should receive, or how it was spent. In such a situation inefficiency
and corruption were virtually invited. Indeed, while venality was
common in Europe at this time, western visitors were frequently
astonished at the scale of corruption they found in Russia. It is possible that well over half of the revenue raised in Russia was stolen by
the officials who handled it.

Initially Peter showed little interest in this administrative chaos;
nor did he seem to realise how urgently the system required reform if
Russia was to mobilise resources on the same scale possible to western
powers. However, in 1699 he realised that if he were to go to war
with Sweden he needed a more reliable system of raising revenue.
He therefore established the *Ratusha* or *Burmistrskaia palata*
(Burgomasters – elected representatives of artisans and merchants –
chamber). This was a central office controlling the revenues collected

by *burmisters* (burghers), elected by the wealthier merchants, who were responsible for collecting the increasingly important taxes from Russian manufacturers and merchants. It took control of the revenue raising powers of 13 different *prikazy* and received all the taxes paid by the cities. The *Ratusha* developed into a central treasury. It also involved reforms of local town governments, which we shall examine later (see page 75). This did not, however, signify a complete break with the past. At the same time Peter established new *prikazy* to undertake new administrative duties for the military. The *Admiralteiskii prikaz*, for example, was responsible for shipyards and shipbuilding.

The speed with which Russia recovered from disaster of Narva might, perhaps, suggest that this new system was not without merit. But it still failed to provide Peter with the funds he demanded. In his desperation for money, he turned increasingly to the *pribylshchiki* (profit-makers), officials whose duty was simply to invent new taxes. Indeed a vast array of new taxes were introduced, including those on beards and moustaches, hats and boots, births and funerals, nuts and melons, firewood and drinking water. New state monopolies were also introduced on a wide range of goods including rhubarb and alcohol, chalk and tar, chessmen and coffins. Yet still he could not raise the money he needed. In 1708, with the Swedish invasion imminent, the inability of the Russian government to supply the quantity of money and recruits Peter required led him to decentralise the administration and divide Russia into eight *gubernii* (governorships), each with its own administration, which we shall examine later (see page 76). For the present, it suffices to say that Peter was mistaken in his assumption that smaller administrative units, supplying money and recruits directly to the army, would prove more efficient than Moscow's unwieldy government system.

3 The Senate

> **KEY ISSUE** Why did the Senate fail to live up to Peter's expectations?

These constant changes had inevitably thrown the central administration of Russia into confusion. Indeed, with the establishment of the *gubernii* many of the *prikazy* no longer had any real function. In short there were no longer any central institutions co-ordinating the administration of Russia. How then was the executive to impose its will on the state? There had been a body which might have undertaken this role – the *Boyars Duma*, the council of leading nobles. But this had long been declining in importance as the Romanov tsars ceased to need its support. Peter had rarely consulted it, and he did not even rely on it to govern Russia when he was absent on the Great Embassy.

Subsequently he ignored it and did not trouble to replace the members who died or retired. Yet his prolonged absences from Moscow made some such decision-making body essential if Russia's government was to function with so many powers devolved on to the *gubernii*.

In February 1711, contemplating another long absence on the Pruth campaign, Peter finally addressed this problem. Initially as a temporary expedient he established the Senate. This was a body of nine members which, in Peter's absence, was to have complete authority to act in his name. It became a permanent institution, concerned with far more than governing Russia while Peter was absent. It was given responsibility for translating Peter's often hurried and cryptic instructions into legislation. It was also made the supreme court of justice. Furthermore, it had the vital duty to 'collect as much money as possible because money is the artery of war'.[2] This in fact did much to reverse Peter's previous decentralisation of Russian government. It had also to fulfil the numerous extra duties assigned to it by Peter, ranging from recruiting nobles into the army to examining trade. Superficially, at least, this appears the type of body which Peter needed to govern Russia effectively. But how effective was it? Was the great authority it theoretically wielded any more than a sham?

One of the Senate's major problems was surely the massive scope of its duties. Even as Peter was blithely piling more tasks upon it, the Senate could not cope with the responsibilities it already held. Perhaps, we could argue, Peter did much to undermine his creation from its inception. There were, furthermore, few men in Russia qualified for such responsibilities. Nor were the Senators chosen from among Peter's closest attendants and favourites: in fact they were aware that they had no power over this entourage. Peter frequently overrode its authority by using his own henchmen to deal with urgent problems. Indeed he also displayed in his treatment of the Senate a failing which he carried throughout his reign – his inability to realise that he could not expect his officials to use their initiative and take responsibilities if they were liable to be harshly punished for making mistakes. The knowledge that they could be flogged – or worse – for mistakes would hardly encourage the Senators to show initiative. Nor could it improve the public standing of their office.

Far from being the efficient organ of government he wanted, Peter's Senate was made up of overworked and inefficient officials who feared taking responsibility and avoided making decisions whenever possible. It was also riven by personal feuds, and its meetings frequently degenerated into violent squabbles. The weaknesses of his Senate were soon made obvious to Peter. In October 1717 he returned from his second trip to the west. While he had been away 'the government of Russia had functioned badly. Maladministration, jealousies and corruption had all but swamped the governmental system he had tried to erect; men who were supposed to be the leaders of the state were quarrelling like children, frantically accusing one another of political and financial misdeeds.'[3] So time-consuming was the investigation into the offences of the Senators that a special court, composed of officers of the Guards, was appointed to deal with the matter. In short, 'things were come to such a pass in Russia, that the members of a venerable Senate, composed of the heads of the greatest families in … [Russia], were obliged to appear before a Lieutenant as their judge, and be called to an account of their conduct.'[4]

Peter attempted to improve efficiency by installing a Procurator General of the Senate, responsible for keeping the body in order and making it reach decisions; but this, together with Peter's frequent reprimands, did little to enhance the prestige of the institution. Nor did having two Senators flogged and their tongues burned for embezzlement help – brutal corporal punishment was common in Russia, but generally only for peasants. Nor did it answer the real problems of the Senate: it was still an overworked body lacking members adequate for their responsibilities. By 1722 a backlog of 16,000 unresolved matters had built up. Peter had little choice but to relieve the Senate of many of its duties, such as initiating legislation, making it a far more limited body than the one he had envisaged.

4 The Colleges

> **KEY ISSUE** What did Peter intend the Colleges to do, and did he succeed?

The need for a more carefully thought-out, systematic and rationally constructed administrative organisation was clear. From around early 1715, when the risk of defeat had receded, Peter began to give this matter serious attention. His attention was drawn to the Swedish system of government, which was, after all, coping remarkably well with the several years' absence of Charles XII, and was still keeping Sweden fighting despite the defeat at Poltava. The Swedish system that Peter largely copied was a collegial system: there was a rational division of administrative responsibilities between a small number of colleges, or ministries. These were under the control of a board, sitting under the chairmanship of a president. Decisions were to be made collectively. This, Peter hoped, would greatly reduce the risk of corruption, nepotism and the domination of a single official, a serious consideration as it was from his close entourage that the first presidents were drawn. Instead all questions would be discussed fully and rational decisions reached. In 1718 the 35 *prikazy* were replaced with nine Colleges of Foreign Affairs, Justice, War, Admiralty, Revenue Collection, Expenditure, Financial Control, Commerce, and of Mining and Manufacturing. The College system represented a far more rational and efficient division of administrative responsibilities, but it had its problems.

Severe personnel difficulties persisted. Lacking any alternative, the Colleges employed the same staff as the old *prikazy*. Just as in the Senate, officials in the Colleges lacked real authority, and fearing punishment for mistakes they proved just as adept at avoiding showing the initiative and energy that their posts, and Peter, required. A number of foreigners were needed to teach the Russian presidents and staff of the Colleges how to operate the new system. At a time when all European governments were expanding their own administrations, and experienced administrators could easily find employment elsewhere, this was a serious problem for Russia. Even among the thousands of Swedish prisoners in Russia only ten (seven of whom were from the Baltic provinces) were willing to serve. Perhaps even more difficult was the entirely alien nature of the system to the Russians, who simply could not understand the terminology of their foreign advisers or the reasons for the procedures they were ordered to adopt. Taking minutes was regarded with deep suspicion by men long accustomed to avoiding responsibility for failures. Thus many of the presidents seem to have had little real idea of the responsibilities and powers of their offices. Also a modern, efficient and honest bureaucracy required that civil servants be paid well, and paid regularly. But Russian rulers, before and after Peter, were perpetually hampered by severely limited resources, and so this proved impossible. Corruption, the Russian custom of *kormlenie* (feeding), still flourished. As we shall see (page 77), another crucial weakness of the system was the lack of local institutions capable of supporting it. Local officials were either baffled or hostile to the system, sending reports which failed to supply the information needed, or so confused that they could not be categorised in St Petersburg. As foreigners in the Colleges were replaced by Russians, collective decision-making increasingly gave way to personal control by their presidents – they became, in short, very much like the *prikazy* they had replaced.

Despite all these shortcomings, the Colleges were a definite improvement in Russia's administration, but perhaps the experiences of the College of Revenue Collection show their limits. In order to draw up a budget it needed information from local authorities concerning the amount of revenue raised locally, as well as their expenses. Yet it proved impossible to collect this information. Local officials lacked the training to understand what was needed or how it could be found. Moreover they had no great desire to provide the government with information which would make their own financial misdeeds easier to uncover. Local officials proved skilled in avoiding providing the College with details, despite some being visited by guards officers with orders to put them in chains until they did. The College never could draw up a budget based on reliable information. This inability to collect information about revenue led to difficulties in collecting the revenue itself. Thus the Senate heard complaints that:

1 the stipulated monies are not being sent to the localities from the [College of Revenue Collection] ... at the predetermined times, for which reason at these locations, namely the army regiments ... the naval troops ... and the rest of the civil servants are suffering unbear-
5 able distress, in addition to which an extensive stoppage ... has come about in the fulfilment of the various duties expected of the other colleges and chancelleries, as well as in connection with orders and purchases.[5]

Of course blaming the College of Revenue Collection for every failure would be very convenient for the other Colleges, but the implications we must surely draw are that Peter's most intensely thought out reform had problems from its inception. He lacked reliable and competent personnel, the system was too alien for most Russians to operate efficiently, there was not the resources to encourage honesty and efficiency, and perhaps in local government there were serious shortcomings which hampered the operation of the system.

5 Local Government Reforms

KEY ISSUE Did Peter merely make a chaotic system more chaotic?

At the start of Peter's reign local affairs in Russia were in the hands of appointed *voevody* (military governors) whose main duties included collecting taxes, organising military mobilisation and administering justice. They were notorious for their avarice. Indeed Peter's motives in establishing the *Ratusha* – the institution collecting revenue from the towns – included taking tax collection out of their hands in the hope that more of the money raised in Peter's name would actually reach him. The *voevody* were to be replaced by *burmistry* (burgomasters), officials elected by artisans and traders who were formed into guilds. But did this reform signal a fundamental change in local government in Russia? Answerable to the *Ratusha* in St Petersburg, the *burmistry* were not trusted with any real autonomy. They were to be the servants of the state, not the representatives of local interests. Originally Peter intended that the towns could free themselves from *voevody* rule by electing *burmistry* and paying double their normal tax for the privilege. But Russia did not have a tradition of elected and unpaid public service. Local administration was seen as either an opportunity to get rich at public expense or as an onerous burden, fraught with risks, because officials were personally responsible for any local shortcomings in revenue. Few were willing to take advantage of Peter's generosity. He subsequently made elected officials compulsory. But unwilling and untrained *burmistry* were not necessarily either more efficient or more honest. In short the corruption and inefficiency of the *voevody* were continued by the *burmistry*.

As Charles XII launched his long feared attack on Russia in 1708, Peter was driven to desperate straits. His reformed local administration simply could not meet his demands for yet more men and money. He undertook a massive decentralisation of Russia, in the hope that separately administered territories would prove more efficient in supporting the specific military units for which they were made directly responsible. In 1708 the *burmistry* were replaced by the eight (eventually 12) *gubernii* (governorships). These vast territories were to be administered with a wide degree of autonomy. The governors he chose from his closest entourage. Menshikov, for example, was appointed to the St Petersburg *gubernia*. This was a mistake, because these were men who already had many other duties, especially military, and they could neither reside in their *gubernia* nor attend to their affairs adequately. In practice they had to deputise officials to run each *uezd* (district), which in practice meant a return to the *voevody*. The evils in local administration which Peter intended to eradicate were still perpetuated. In 1715 a further administrative unit was introduced, the *doli* (fractions), an area to cover an average of 5,536 peasant households (a figure arbitrarily selected by Peter for no readily apparent reason), generally differing territorially from the *uezd*. These were intended to be administered by provincial councillors, making decisions collectively. But yet again practice differed from intention, and the councillors were subordinate to the governors. Indeed *voevody*, renamed *kommendants*, were as much in power as ever.

In practice the *gubernii* proved to be too large to be administered as efficiently as Peter had hoped. Eventually Peter accepted this, and yet another reform was instituted. In May 1719 the *gubernii* were replaced by 50 *provintsii* (provinces). These were intended, following the Swedish model, to have elected councillors to advise the governors. But in practice they were appointed by either the governor or the Senate. Thus any form of local supervision of the governors was lost. All the problems which had dogged reforms of the central government were to be found in local administration. Most important was the lack of adequate personnel to administer the new institutions. The best of the nobles were in government service already; only the retired and the shirkers were left to manage local affairs. Corruption, nepotism and incompetence remained as rife as they had always been. Also Peter simply did not have the resources to implement his reforms properly. He spent less on local administration than the Swedes did on Livonia alone. Nor were his constant changes helpful. In Russian local administration the situation was confused further in

1724 by the introduction of the *polkovoi distrikt* (regimental district), with wide powers in tax collecting and conscription, which overlapped or cut across provincial boundaries. These were the quartering areas which supported each regiment. The army had special duties in collecting the poll tax and rounding up runaway serfs. In practice the military became predominant in local administration.

Local administration remained arbitrary, as did the provision of justice. Peter proved unable to produce a new law code, despite ordering it done three times. Russian law had last been codified in 1649. Since then a vast number of *ukazy* (decrees) especially from Peter himself, had massively complicated the law. Peter was never willing to give this problem the attention necessary to solve it. He had attempted to introduce civil courts in every *gubernia*, but the interference of local officials stopped them becoming effective. Criminal law was left to military statute: a very harsh and despotic method of dispensing justice. Did his failure to see the importance of this offer a further explanation for the difficulties his administrative reforms encountered? The Swedish system he was trying to introduce into Russia was based, ultimately, upon the rule of law and the consent of the populace. But the lowest Swedish administrative unit, equivalent to the parish, was not copied by Peter. The involvement of a free peasantry at the lowest level was the basic building block of the Swedish system. But in Russia the peasants were serfs, who could not be entrusted with involvement in local government. The central aim of Peter's reforms was, after all, not to make Russia better governed but to squeeze money and service out of the populace. Perhaps this was a basic flaw which undermined both local and central government reforms. Claes Peterson argues very strongly that, lacking an equivalent to the parish unit, Russian local administration 'was unable to develop methods of operation corresponding to those of its Swedish prototype, and this in turn detracted from the ability of the colleges to carry out their various responsibilities'.[6] Should we not therefore conclude that in his local government reforms, all Peter produced was administrative chaos and that the institutions he imposed did not long survive him?

6 The Church Reform

> **KEY ISSUE** Did Peter reduce the Church to his service?

At first glance it might seem odd to consider Church reforms alongside those of government. But Peter treated the Russian Orthodox Church more as a department of government than as an institution responsible only for the care of souls. As we shall see (page 100), his offences against religious sensibilities were bitterly resented. But Peter remained devoutly Orthodox, if tolerant of other sects – he believed

FEOFAN PROKOPOVICH (1681–1736)

The Ukrainian born theologian who became one of Peter's most steadfast collaborators. He studied at the Kiev Academy. This institution, the best available to the Russian Orthodox Church, trained priests to face the Counter-Reformation missionary zeal of the Jesuits. Wanting to further his studies, however, Prokopovich knew that there was no institution outside Rome capable of meeting his needs. He therefore became a member of the Uniate Church, which followed the Orthodox ritual but accepted the authority of the Pope. Upon his return he reverted to Orthodoxy. But as far as many Russian conservatives were concerned, he was forever a heretic.

He taught literature and rhetoric, as well as theology, at the Kiev Academy. But he attracted Peter's attention through his flattering preaching. In 1716 he was summoned to St Petersburg, where his support for Peter proved invaluable, and was made Archbishop of Pskov in 1718. Whatever step Peter took Prokopovich would support from the pulpit. When Alexis was brought to trial (see page 107), for example, he preached on obedience to the sovereign. He was a enthusiastic supporter of education reforms and of westernisation in general, helping in the foundation of the Russian Academy of Science. He contributed much to the Ecclesiastical Regulation and aided the establishment of the Holy Synod, putting the Church at the service of the state. It was Prokopovich who tearfully delivered Peter's funeral oration (see page 4).

faith was more important than the form of religious service. He also wanted the clergy to be useful, especially in teaching and saving souls. He had no patience with the large number of idle and ignorant priests he saw in Russia. He was also enraged by superstitions he believed they perpetuated. He took determined steps to reduce the numbers of monks and nuns. The young and fit, he held, should be employed usefully serving the state. He eventually decreed that no man under 50 could become a monk. He also felt that the vast wealth of the monasteries would also be better employed in the service of the state.

More important to Peter, however, was the great authority of this intensely conservative institution. The Russian Patriarch had been treated as equals by previous tsars. Patriarch Adrian, for example, interfered in Peter's own private life, criticising his appearance, his friends and his treatment of his wife, Eudoxia. When Adrian died in 1700, Peter wanted a replacement more in sympathy with his views. He therefore appointed Stefan Yavorsky, an educated Ukrainian cleric, as Exarch (temporary guardian) of the Russian Orthodox Church, a title with much less prestige than Patriarch. This was also a move which allowed easier access to the great revenue of the monasteries, and the *Monastyrskii Prikaz* was formed to administer (meaning appropriate) them. But Yavorsky was not one of Peter's unconditional supporters and could be critical himself. It was in another learned Ukrainian cleric, Feofan Prokopovich, that Peter found a churchman who was prepared, either from conviction or opportunism, to subordinate the Church to the state, and indeed provide a justification for any step Peter wanted to take. He was the principal architect of the Ecclesiastical Regulation of 1721. This attacked superstition and ignorance, especially among priests. It also abolished the Patriarchate, replacing it with the Most Holy All-Ruling Synod, a collegiate body under the supervision of a lay procurator, often an army officer. In short the Church's independence was destroyed and it was reduced to a department of state.

Where the reforms of Alexei and Nikon had led to schism and defiance, however, there was no resistance to Peter's reforms. The hierarchy of the Church were individually browbeaten into acquiescing and the Russian people were indifferent. Peter was, after all, attacking the Church's administration, not the dogma and ritual that Russians treasured. In the long term, Peter's reforms caused some improvement in the standards of the parish clergy, but with its independence the Church lost its dynamism. Peter now demanded that Priests who heard treasonous or criminal confessions should report them. This seems to have been generally ignored. But the tax exemptions of the clergy and the demands that they act as government agents 'undoubtedly worked to identify them with the increasingly oppressive state and thus divide them from the people they served'.[7]

7 Conclusion

> **KEY ISSUE** Did Peter establish absolute rule in Russia?

Certainly, if we define absolutism as the exercise of unlimited centralised power by the monarch, Peter was an absolute monarch. He tolerated no institutional checks on his power. All the institutions he established, from the Senate to the *doli*, were to serve his will, not represent the interests of any social or geographical section of Russia. But, of course, we must realise that his predecessors would tolerate no such checks either. In Russia the idea of autocracy (unrestricted rule by the sovereign) long predated Peter. This autocracy was only temporarily weakened by the Time of Troubles. There was, however, one major change instituted by Peter. Russia's Patriarch had great prestige and moral authority, and could, as we have seen (page 79), criticise the tsar. This was ended by Peter. Subordinating the Church to the state was unquestionably an absolutist step. But was it really a fundamental change? The position of the Patriarch depended on the personal piety of the tsars. If the tsar was angered by his Patriarch, as Alexei was angered by Nikon (see page 15), it was the Patriarch who suffered. Peter was a devout Orthodox Christian but had little respect for the priesthood. Perhaps his only real reform was to put the Church formally and publicly at the service of the state. Could we not then say that Peter did not introduce absolutism into Russia, but concluded a development which had been in progress for a very long time?

Perhaps we should consider absolutism in terms of a government machinery more effective in ensuring that its orders were obeyed? Certainly in comparison with the administrative chaos of the *prikazy* system, Peter constructed a far more efficient system. Even if there was still a degree of overlapping functions and confusion how to work the College system, at least it was clearer where responsibilities lay. Yet Peter never eradicated corruption despite all his efforts. Also, as we shall see (page 101), passive resistance to Peter frustrated many of his aims. Perhaps we might conclude that in these terms Peter's ability to impose his will on Russia was far less successful than it might superficially appear.

References

1 John Perry, *The State of Russia under the Present Czar* (Frank Cass, 1967), pp. 261–263.
2 Decree on the duties of the Senate, Basil Dmytryshyn (ed.), *Imperial Russia: a Source Book* (The Dryden Press, Hinsdale, 1974), p.14.
3 Robert K. Massie, *Peter the Great: His Life and World* (Gollancz, 1981), p. 657.
4 Friedrich Christian Weber, *The Present State of Russia, vol. 1* (Frank Cass, 1968), p. 193.
5 Claes Peterson, *Peter the Great's Administrative and Judicial Reforms* (A.-B. Nordiska Bokhandeln, Stockholm, 1979), p. 174.
6 Peterson, *Peter the Great's Administrative and Judicial Reforms*, p. 414.
7 James Cracraft, *The Church Reform of Peter the Great* (Macmillan, 1971), p. 251.

Working on chapter 5

Summary Diagram
Transforming the government

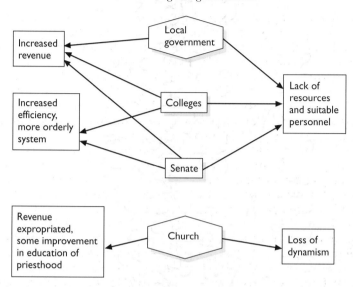

Source-based questions on Chapter 5

1 Peter's paradise: St Petersburg
Read the section on St Petersburg, and in particular the extract from Perry on pages 68–9, and study the illustrations of St Petersburg and Moscow on pages 67 and 69. Answer the following questions.

a) What do the illustrations tell us were the main differences between Moscow and St Petersburg? (*5 marks*)
b) Why, according to Perry, was St Petersburg disliked? (*5 marks*)
d) What was Peter attempting to achieve with his new capital? (*10 marks*)

Hints and advice: Pictorial sources need to be treated with the same rigour as written sources. Remember that, like written sources, they were deliberately produced to convey specific impressions. Also you must remember that we today will perceive these impressions differently than would contemporaries. How did the Russians of Peter's age see the two cities? Parts a) and b) are fairly straightforward. Part c) invites you to use your knowledge of Peter and his aims and use the sources to illustrate that understanding.

Answering structured and essay questions on Chapter 5

Questions on this topic do sometimes appear. Examples include the following:

1. **a)** What were the main features of Peter's reforms of central government?
   b) How far did these reforms amount to a fundamental reform of Russian government?
2. To what extent did Peter the Great use foreigners and western-style reforms to strengthen his absolute rule?

In the first section of question one, remember the importance of brevity and relevance. In the following section, where a more analytical approach is required, you need to compare what Peter had introduced with what had existed before. Also bring into your discussion the limitations of these reforms. What were the main problems: personnel, finance, the alien nature of the system, etc? Once you have summarised the strengths and weaknesses of the two systems, try to reach a clear conclusion.

It is, of course, essential for question 2 that you have a very clear idea of what you mean by 'absolutism'. Also you must address the question of how absolutely Russia had been ruled before Peter came to the throne. Did he really change Russia's style of rule? Consider the major institutional reforms: do they in any way strengthen absolutism? Church reform will obviously be prominent in your analysis. Why do foreigners enter the question? Are they irrelevant, or should we see absolutism as being strengthened by being made more efficient?

6 Transforming Russian Society

POINTS TO CONSIDER

Did Peter make a new Russia, or new Russians? This chapter will introduce you to the main economic and social reforms of Peter the Great. A crucial debate about his reign is whether his reforms in this field made a fundamental change to Russia. Try to assess whether the evidence suggests they were fundamental or only superficial.

KEY DATES

1696 First Russians sent to the west to learn seamanship.
1698 Russian nobles ordered to shave and wear western clothes.
1700 Julian Calendar adopted.
1714 Decrees on education of the nobility and inheritance.
1719 St Petersburg Naval Academy founded.
1724 Russian Academy of Science founded.

In order to fight his wars Peter was forced to extract more than just money and service from his people, he had to build an industrial base to support his new armed forces and to generate even greater wealth. As we have already seen (page 30), he wanted to make Russia a seafaring nation as well. He also sought to make the services he extracted from his nobility more effective through compulsory education. He demanded that all Russians serve the state. The nobility were to give lifelong service in the armed forces or bureaucracy, while the peasantry were to bear ever greater burdens and obligations, culminating in their reduction to a state of serfdom often seen as equivalent to slavery. But, while war was the main impetus for Peter's reforms, should we assume that it was the only impetus? Did Peter have a wider vision of Russia's future, so that he wanted a Russia which could meet the west on equal terms, economically and culturally, as well as politically? Indeed, can his early moves to force his nobles to shave and adopt western dress be explained in any other terms?

1 Cultural and Social Innovations

> **KEY ISSUE** Why did Peter make his nobility adopt western culture?

Peter certainly wanted Russia to have the power of western nations. But did he also want to import the institutions which gave the west the cultural ascendancy he recognised? He was quick to abandon some of the more obviously medieval customs of the court of Moscow. He stopped his nobles referring to themselves as his *kholops* (slaves). Upon his return from the Great Embassy he shocked Russia by forcing his nobles to shave off their beards and adopt western clothes. For a nation long convinced of its moral superiority such a move was not just incomprehensible, it was humiliating. Shaving was especially distressing. Russians considered their beards a gift from God, and hence to shave might well destroy their chances of salvation. But Peter cared nothing for the offence he caused. Other reforms were intended to make Russia conform with the west. He abolished the traditional Russian calendar, decreeing that Russians must celebrate the new year of 1700 on 1 January, instead of the new year of 7208 on the following 1 September. (Yet he adopted the Julian calendar at a time when the west was beginning to abandon it for the Gregorian version.) He also reformed the alphabet, allowing the development of secular literature. There was a great increase in the number of books published, both secular and religious, and a journal, *vedomosti*, appeared. Of course, as Lindsay Hughes points out, that does not necessarily mean that more books were read, but their possession did symbolise western modernity.

Peter was also credited with emancipating noble women from the *terem* (secluded quarters). He certainly did demand that the wives and daughters of his nobles take a more public role. They too were required to adopt western fashions and had to take part in mixed sex social events. In 1718 he issued a *ukaz*, compelling his nobles to hold assemblies – informal social events in their own homes, at which both men and women could mix freely. He also banned arranged marriages and took some steps to improve women's property rights. But can we assume that he had any strong interest in improving the social position of women? He did little to change Russian divorce customs. This, perhaps, is not too surprising, as he had followed Russian tradition to rid himself of his first wife, Eudoxia, by forcing her to become a nun – a move of questionable validity as she was definitely unwilling. Perhaps Peter was simply attempting to introduce into St Petersburg the practices of polite society he had witnessed in the west. The conduct of his court was certainly an important standard by which foreigners judged Russia's worth. His steps to establish an art gallery, library, museums and ultimately the Academy of Science might be seen in the same light. The west had such institutions; and if Russia was to face the west as an equal, Russia must have them also. Similarly, if western courts included women in polite society, Russian women must conform to such customs.

Nor should we assume that Peter's innovations were universally welcomed by women. Russian noble women were unprepared in their upbringing for the role Peter demanded. They were required to adopt fashions which many must have found immodest if not indecent. Peter's demands must surely have caused considerable distress. Nor was Peter himself consistent in improving the standing of his court. The antics of the Drunken Synod continued to scandalise foreigners and Russians alike. Peter's often crude sense of humour could lead him to excesses involving the women of his court also. It was not unusual for them to be forced to drink vast quantities of alcohol. Only the outraged opposition of the nobility prevented him sending their daughters abroad to study as he sent their sons, where they would 'be led into temptation and their virtue and reputations endangered'.[1] Women could find life in St Petersburg very unpleasant indeed. But Peter would make far more drastic demands upon Russia in order to turn it into a formidable power. He also recognised the need for an economy capable of underpinning such pretensions.

2 Economic Reforms

KEY ISSUE What were the flaws in Peter's economic reforms?

a) Military considerations

Military considerations were often foremost in Peter's mind when he showed an interest in economic affairs. After the disaster at Narva (1700) his desperate need to replace the weapons he had lost, especially the artillery, was to give a boost to the development of Russia's metallurgy industry. Immediate expedients, such as melting down Church bells, were no long-term solution to Peter's military needs. He therefore ordered surveys of the Urals for new mineral deposits, which found valuable copper as well as iron ore. Between 1701 and 1704 seven new iron works were opened in the region. Existing foundries were also expanded, and 52 new ones opened during the reign, some of them very large and well-equipped. His ruthless determination to increase production led him to brush aside property rights. A *ukaz* of 1719 gave anyone the right to exploit mineral deposits, even on the land of another if the owner failed to exploit them. He also made it a criminal offence for nobles to conceal the existence of mineral wealth on their lands. By Peter's death Russia had 16,000 cannon held in reserve. But his success was in more than simply producing cannon. There was a dramatic rise in iron production, so much so that by 1716 Russia was a net exporter of iron. In 1700 Russia had produced 150,000 *poods* of pig iron, and had imported the metal; by Peter's death production had risen to 800,000 *poods*, and by the middle of the century Russia became the world's largest exporter. (1 *pood* = 16.3 kg.)

Metallurgy was not the only industry to benefit by serving Peter's war needs, the textile and leather industries were expanded to meet his needs for uniforms, sails and saddles. Of course, we must not make the mistake of assuming that Russian industrialisation was entirely due to Peter's intervention. Previous tsars had accepted the military importance of a domestic metal industry. During the 1630s foreigners established iron works at Tula. There were probably over 20 manufacturies, mostly related to metallurgy, in Russia at the start of Peter's reign. He had the advantage of his predecessor's work, but that was very limited, and the expansion he encouraged was impressive.

b) Mercantilist influences

Peter had ambitions far beyond simply improving Russia's arms industries, important though these were. He also subscribed to mercantilist views, which were popular in Europe at the time. Such views suggested that the wealth of a nation depended on the possession of precious metals. Therefore to keep them in the country, imports, which drained wealth, must be kept low and exports encouraged. Also colonies were desirable, as sources of raw materials and markets. To this end Peter sent expeditions to central Asia, one of which founded the town of Omsk. He also annexed Kamchatka and the Kurile Islands, territory which was in size, if not in value, greater than he conquered in all of his wars. In the last weeks of his life he sent Vitus Bering to discover if Siberia and the Americas were connected. But mercantilism also required that a nation develop its own merchant marine. This Peter failed to do, not least because the British and the Dutch were determined to maintain their control on Baltic shipping, and also because no Russian entrepreneurs could be interested in such a project. Peter, we might conclude, recognised that a nation's military might depended ultimately upon its prosperity. Having seen first-hand the wealth and power of the Dutch and British, he probably wanted the same for Russia. He certainly developed grandiose dreams of diverting oriental trade through St Petersburg. But little came from his negotiations with China to that end. He even ordered an abortive naval expedition to Madagascar as a stepping stone to India (see page 59).

c) Communications

Peter also recognised that Russia, severely hampered by its vast size, was served by very poor communications. The construction of St Petersburg merely underlined how slow and expensive transporting goods was over Russia's abysmally poor roads. Even before the war with Sweden he ordered the construction of a new canal system. These were ambitious projects, which included a plan to connect the

Volga and Don rivers, which would give access between the Caspian and Azov seas. After 10 years of great effort and cost the project was abandoned when Peter lost Azov. But by 1709, after similar exertions, the Neva and Volga rivers were connected, and soon 2,000 tons of freight were travelling along this route annually. In 1718 Peter decided to have a 65 mile canal built to bypass lake Ladoga, where shipping losses through storms were heavy. This was not completed until 1732, largely because of the mismanagement of Menshikov, who was originally in charge of the project, and later, when he was replaced, by his obstruction – he had no desire to see another succeed where he had failed. The canal system Peter envisaged, linking the Black, Caspian White and Baltic seas, was only completed during the following century. But at least the first steps had been taken. Whether the efforts and resources expended, amidst so much waste, were worth the results, is, of course, open to debate.

d) Importing expertise

Peter was also interested in industries which were only relevant to his military needs through the taxable wealth they were intended to produce. He established silk, ribbon, and velvet industries as well as brickworks and papermills. These he protected with high tariffs. Indeed in 1724 he set a tariff on a wide range of goods at 50 to 75 per cent of their value. One observer, Peter Bruce, noted approvingly that before Peter, Russia:

1 shipped yearly great quantities of hemp to all parts of Europe, yet they were obliged to bring their sail-cloth and cordage, manufactured abroad, from their own hemp. To remedy this evil the czar erected manufactures for sail-cloth, and rope-walks ... and that nothing might
5 be wanting for the improvement of his country, skilful miners were got from Hungary and Saxony, who discovered metals of all sorts. ... It was surprising to see so many great things undertaken, and put in execution by one single person, without the assistance and help of any one.[2]

Others, such as John Perry, saw failures. He reported that Peter spent a great fortune attempting to set up a woollen industry, building and equipping a factory and importing hundreds of Dutch experts:

1 before the experiment of making one yard of cloth was produced; and when it came to be fully try'd, it was found that the Russ wooll, which is very short, and as coarse almost as dogs hair, would not make any thread for cloth; so that afterward they were obliged to send to Holland
5 for wooll to mix with it; and at the foot of the whole account, it is found that even such coarse cloth, as has been made only fit for soldiers, can be deliver'd much easier to the Czar, than to have it made in Russia.[3]

Perry also expressed surprise that Peter paid little attention to Russia's linen industry, which he thought could have been greatly and profitably improved with far less expense and effort. There were other failures in Peter's projects. The silk factory he subsidised failed due to the mismanagement and quarrels of his confederates, Apraxin, Tolstoy, Shafirov and Menshikov, who controlled the project. One problem was that Peter, in his enthusiasm to establish new industries, paid little attention to initial costs. This provided great opportunities for his closest associates, and even his more obscure servants, to line their pockets. Also his schemes were continually impeded by a lack of skilled labour. Peter went to great lengths to recruit foreign experts, promising, if not always delivering, very high wages. He also sent many Russians abroad to learn skills. He was, however, often ill-served by foreigners, who were frequently willing to take his money but had no intention of spreading knowledge of craft secrets to potential competitors. The trainees he sent abroad often had little interest in the skills they were meant to learn and stubbornly resisted attempts to educate them. Indeed, Peter's representative in London complained that the Russian students there refused to learn, and he had no powers to punish them under English law. Some of these students developed an interest in western culture, which might be seen as the origins of Russia's westernised cultural elite – indeed as the origins of the revolutionary intelligentsia of the 19th century. This, however, was hardly Peter's intention.

e) The role of the State

Peter soon found that if he wanted Russians to develop industry, he would have to use both incentives and force. Through his personal intervention, later using the College of Mining and Manufacture, the state provided the initial capital, even building the factories and granting privileges, such as monopolies, subsidies and tax exemptions, and permission to buy villages for serf labour. Then he would compel individuals or groups to lease them. Even given these advantages, industries could still fail. They were often required to produce for the state, at the state's prices, which allowed very limited opportunities for profit and involved extremely harsh punishments for failure. Taxes remained very high for most industrialists, which made it very difficult to accumulate investment capital. Peter recognised the need for entrepreneurs, accepting that the state could not provide all of Russia's economic needs. Part of his problem was that his nobility despised trade. Russian merchants were notorious for their dishonesty. But the problem was more fundamental. By and large merchants and industrialists remained at the mercy of the *voevody* (the notoriously grasping military governors). They proved reluctant to take risks. Russia's lack of common justice, and the arbitrariness of local officials, had long meant that Russians were very reluctant to be recognised as conspicuously successful. That simply invited expropriation. Instead of investing their wealth, Russians tended to hoard it, and some of the more resourceful nobles were beginning to bank abroad.

The result of this was that Peter's drive to introduce industry in his country unavoidably gave the state an excessive role in Russian economic life. This we might argue stifled the development of an entrepreneurial class. The charters and privileges, the dependency on servile labour and state contracts, which Peter used to foster industry, actually undermined enterprise. Rather than nurturing enterprise, he reinforced a pattern of dependency on the state. Thus Peter had very limited success in promoting private enterprise. He could not overcome Russia's basic problems: the absence of any tradition of enterprise, its lack of private capital and a backward labour force. Serfdom, furthermore, prevented the emergence of any free class of skilled artisans. Nor did it permit the growth of a significant domestic market. Peter certainly increased industrial production, but he did not introduce capitalism to Russia. Few of his people proved adept at grasping the possibilities offered by his policies. A rare exception was Nikita Demidov, an illiterate artisan from Tula, whose foundry business grew until he was the foremost industrialist in Russia. He was ennobled for his successes in 1720. But the source of his wealth was government contracts. Ultimately even he, like other successful industrialists, depended upon the state and his influence over it, rather than his entrepreneurial skills, to prosper.

How then are we to perceive Peter's economic reforms? There was certainly a dramatic increase in investment and output. By the end of his reign 233 factories and workshops were established. Some did collapse after Peter's death, especially from a reduction in military orders. Several, however, survived, especially in the fields of metallurgy and mining. Also some light industries in the Moscow region, including linen and leather, continued to prosper. Foreign trade increased four-fold during Peter's reign, with a large trade balance in Russia's favour. Trade and industry were seen by the state less as reserves to be bled dry, and more as a resource to be nurtured and protected. Indeed M.S. Anderson suggests that Peter's 'economic policies were as intelligent, as consistent and as successful as those of any ruler of the age in western Europe'.[4] Nevertheless he failed to bring into existence the class of independent entrepreneurs he wanted, and which he felt to be essential to Russia's development. Was this as an omission far outweighing any increase in the volume of goods Russia produced? Peter forced a group of industrialists into being, but he could not make them function in precisely the way he envisaged. Should we not ask whether, once again, a shortage of adequate personnel limited his reforms?

3 The Services of the Nobility

> **KEY ISSUE** How successful was Peter in mobilising the nobility to his service?

There was nothing new in Russia in the idea that the nobility should serve the state. Indeed service from the age of 15 years was the norm. By the 16th century the *boyars* were already being outnumbered by a new class of nobles whose land and titles depended upon service: the *dvoryanstvo* (service nobility). But service was commonly intermittent, and often confined to wartime, and even then there had been considerable evasion. Peter extended his demands for service and made them universal. Unlike his predecessors, he needed a large number of professional army and navy officers competent in modern tactics and equipment. Evasion could no longer be tolerated. A *ukaz* of 1712 demanded that all sons of nobles report to the Senate for assignment to the army or navy. In 1714 all noblemen aged 10 to 30 were ordered to register for service. But Peter's demands were not only more sweeping, they called for more arduous service. Now nobles were required to enter the army as privates and earn their commissions. This hardly suited their long tradition of military leadership, and was resented. Those assigned to the navy considered themselves exceptionally unfortunate, as sea-service was universally detested. Strenuous efforts were made to avoid military service by entering the civil service, which was not only less hazardous and uncomfortable, but also offered the chance of rich pickings. But Peter quickly limited entry to the civil service to one third of a family. He went on to threaten shirkers with outlawry, which would mean that they could be robbed or killed freely. He also established the office of *Heraldmeister*, to keep records of the nobility and ensure that none evaded service.

He also overturned custom by decreeing a new law on inheritance, which ended the practice of dividing an inheritance between all sons. This not only impoverished a family within a few generations, it allowed younger sons to live idly. In a *ukaz* of March 1714 Peter ordered that henceforth landowners were to chose a single heir, not necessarily the eldest but, insofar as this was possible, the ablest. Peter intended that this law should end the impoverishment of families, and also force the other sons into state service. Yet the rule was utterly hated: it caused bitter family feuds, and was widely evaded, if not simply ignored. It also greatly complicated property rights, and was revoked soon after Peter's death. But it did bring to an end the distinction, which was long becoming blurred anyway, between *pomestie* estates (those held by nobles conditionally upon their performing services to the tsar) and *votchina* estates (inherited without conditions). All estates were now inheritable, but all landowners, and their sons, had to serve for life. Perhaps we might argue that the nobility were made into a more homogeneous group, which could henceforth develop collective objectives. But again this was not Peter's aim.

With his greater demand for technical skills we should not be surprised to find that Peter saw education as a vital preparation for state service. Traditionally Russian education was in the hands of the

Church. This meant it was largely limited to supplying a grounding in the gospels and a smattering of literacy for the few who had access to it. In 1701 Peter established the School Mathematics and Navigation, which was moved to St Petersburg in 1715 and called the Naval Academy. This was headed by a Scot, Henry Farquharson. It was Peter's first step in establishing secular education, and was deliberately focused on the technical skills he wanted his nobility to acquire. Yet the School suffered, as did so many of his reforms, through his lack of resources. The teachers were rarely paid, and students, it was claimed, were reduced to begging in the streets. Discipline was harsh, with retired soldiers with whips in the classrooms. Unsurprisingly several students fled. But the School did have successes, producing not just sailors but engineers, architects and teachers. In 1714 Peter decided that all 10 year old nobles were to receive five years of secular education. He ordered the School to supply two students for every province to teach science. By 1722 over 40 such schools had been established. These were the cipher schools. They were to teach young nobles basic arithmetic, geometry, literacy and the scriptures as a preparation for service. These demands provoked much resistance, and the nobles evaded sending their sons. After all, those who performed well risked being ordered into the hated navy. Most of those who sent their sons withdrew them when the lower classes were given access to the schools. Despite Peter forbidding nobles to marry until they had completed their education, he was unable to enforce education. His decree was revoked in 1716. Other classes he tried to drive into schools similarly resisted. Artisans successfully protested that they needed their sons at home to learn their trades. Also the cipher schools faced competition from the ecclesiastical schools Peter ordered opened in the Ecclesiastical regulation of 1721. These were also to teach a wide syllabus, including science, history and logic as well as theology. He compelled bishops to establish one in each diocese. Consequently the sons of clerics transferred there from the cipher schools. Many cipher schools, such as those at Novgorod and Pskov, were left empty.

Essentially Peter had little success in making his nobility accept the education he felt they needed to serve him adequately. Of all pupils at the cipher schools – nobles and others – less than one in five completed the course, and over two-thirds were withdrawn, or fled (or never appeared), or proved to be incapable of learning. Peter failed to establish elementary education in Russia. He was too interested in technical training to perceive the necessity for it. He opened a medical school and language, artillery, engineering and mining colleges, which produced hundreds of specialists. But during his lifetime most of Russia was unaffected by his education reforms. He had, in fact, only provided Russia with the seeds of an education system.

By far the most famous of his moves to mobilise his nobility was

Peter's Table of Ranks. This ordered that all Russians entering the
service of the state enter at bottom and rise through merit.
Henceforth, Peter proclaimed, precedence at court and in office
would depend on the rank earned, not on any title inherited. In
theory nobility of birth, without service, counted for nothing.

Table of Ranks			
Military Ranks		**Civilian Ranks**	**Grades**
Naval Forces	*Land Forces*		
General-Admiral	Geralissimo	Chancellor or Active	I
	Field Marshal	Privy Counsellor	
Admiral	General of Artillery	Active Privy	II
	General of Cavalry	Counsellor	
	General of Infantry		
Vice Admiral	Lieutenant General	Privy Counsellor	III
Rear Admiral	Major General	Active State Counsellor	IV
Captain-Commander	Brigadier	State Counsellor	V
First Captain	Colonel	Collegial Counsellor	VI[5]

There were 14 ranks in all. Those who reached the eighth rank,
Lieutenant-Captain of the Fleet, army Major or Collegial Assessor,
automatically earned hereditary nobility. This included low born
Russians and foreigners.

Should we conclude that Peter was trying to introduce a meritoc-
racy? He was certainly willing to reward talented and energetic supporters and was indifferent to their backgrounds: consider the
rewards he heaped on his second wife, Catherine (see page 99), and
even Menshikov. But the obvious pool of talented and educated
people was the traditional nobility. This, we might argue, was the
group he most wanted to mobilise. By suggesting that their titles
were no longer the main measure of their worth, was he not attempting to spur them into striving to climb this new ladder of ranks, to
preserve their elite status? Perhaps he wanted to enlist the services of
the existing nobility (and perhaps enlarge it somewhat), and had no
real interest in social mobility for its own sake. There was, perhaps,
more continuity than disruption in the top levels of Russian society.
There were indeed great rewards for willing and talented service, but
they were as likely to go to the noble born, men like Boris
Sheremetev, as they were to the low born, like Menshikov. Perhaps
we might view it as a measure of Peter's difficulties that, for all the
powers of compulsion available to him, he was unable to force his
nobles to become the educated and willing servants he desired. Had
he, in fact, no alternative to enticing them into his service by presenting them with a new social hierarchy to climb, and offering substantial inducements? That the inducements offered were substantial

indeed seems certain. They did, after all, include a much tighter control over the peasantry, who can be presented as the main victims of Peter's reign.

4 The Services of the Peasantry

> **KEY ISSUE** In what ways did the peasantry pay for Peter's reforms?

It is a truism that in a pre-industrial society, the only substantial source of wealth is the agricultural sector, in Russia's case, the peasantry. It is also certain that in Russia the lot of the peasant had been declining from the mid 16th century. Access to new lands in Siberia had threatened the security of the landowners, whose workforce moved to the new lands. This led the state to restrict the movement of peasants by imposing serfdom. The burden of taxation and labour demands upon the peasantry had long been onerous. Under Peter they were to multiply. As his needs grew he assigned responsibility for financing his projects in an arbitrary fashion. Thus fixed sums were demanded from peasants in Kazan to pay for the transportation of timber, and from the Church's peasants for dragoons' pay. Further extraordinary demands were made to pay for the fleet. Taxes multiplied and the monopolies he granted pushed up the prices of essentials, the salt monopoly causing much hardship, illness, and death. Forced labour was repeatedly decreed, and thousands were forced to march vast distances to work on Peter's canals and shipyards, on St Petersburg and other projects, generally under terrible conditions. Peasants were assigned to industry, frequently under worse conditions than in agriculture. His commands could devastate communities, as when Charles XII marched on Russia, and Peter ordered a 120 mile wide zone devastated from Pskov to Smolensk (see page 49).

For his first campaign against Narva (1700) Peter demanded that landowners supply one recruit for every 50 serf households in their possession. After that fiasco he decided that he needed a permanent professional standing army. The peasantry were to fill the ranks. Peter established a system of conscription for a 25 year period of service. As we have seen (page 47), this was recognised as a life sentence. During the reign over 300,000 peasants were conscripted. A standing army of over 100,000 was built. But the peasantry were to do more than supply manpower, they were to pay for this enormously costly body. The military was to swallow two-thirds of state revenue even in peacetime. Desperate to increase his revenue, and accepting that indirect taxes could not meet his needs, Peter examined the traditional household tax. He found that it led to much evasion, either through overcrowding to reduce the number of households, concealment by temporarily demolishing huts whenever tax assessors appeared, or simply through bribing officials. He decided in 1718 to replace it with a poll tax on all peasants. The census of 1722 counted 5,794,928 male peasants, and Peter simply divided his estimated needs between them. In 1722 that meant that peasants on private land paid 74 kopecks, and on state land 114 kopecks. This produced half of his revenue needs. But what Peter never took into account was the peasantry's ability to pay.

Furthermore, in order to ensure that the peasants did not evade his taxes through flight, he gave the nobility greater powers over them. In 1722 he decreed that peasants could not leave their estates without written permission, in short introducing the idea of internal passports. He also gave the landowner the obligation of collecting the tax, supported by greater powers to punish insubordination. The need to ensure that all paid made Peter remove distinctions and privileges within the peasantry. He arbitrarily forced a range of classes into one single class of serfs. Degrees of servitude had varied widely, they were now consolidated. The *volnitsy* (free men, generally vagrants and beggars) were forced to chose between being serfs, soldiers or galley slaves, *delovye* (small tradesmen) and *zhilye* (bound as serfs for a limited period) became serfs. So too did *kholops* (slaves), whose status had hitherto exempted them from taxation. All were now numbered among either the state owned peasants or privately owned serfs. For the serfs this was a major blow. As well as being bound to the land, they were now subjected to a personal bondage, which made them, in effect, chattels. They became traded commodities, which Peter disliked but did not prevent. He issued a *ukaz* forbidding selling members of families separately, but took no steps to enforce it. In 1719 he issued a *ukaz* stating that if a landowner caused undue hardships to his serfs, he could lose his estate. This was done in fear of peasant flight and the resulting loss of revenue, not on humanitarian grounds. It appears to have been completely ignored. Even the old practice of serf abduction by nobles seeking more labourers continued, only now it was almost akin to cattle rustling.

Can any positive assessment be made of Peter's policies towards the peasants? The old household tax was essentially a tax on land, a strong disincentive to increase tillage. The poll tax removed that disincentive and acreage under the plough did expand rapidly. But this was unintentional on Peter's part, he only sought to increase revenue. Perhaps his biggest error with the peasantry was being unable to realise that they were not an inexhaustible source of money. Even after Poltava taxes still took 64 per cent of peasant crops. Indeed in 1724, 18 per cent of the poll tax was not collected: it simply could not be paid. Not only had they been reduced to abject servility, the peasants were utterly impoverished. Peter's policy of stationing the army in regimental districts imposed yet another huge burden. The military provided an arbitrary and brutal administration. As we shall see (page 101), the peasants did resist Peter's impositions. Indeed he was widely hated. But were there any practical alternatives for Peter? Could the necessary resources have been extracted with the consent of the peasantry?

5 Conclusion

KEY ISSUE Did Peter instigate any profound changes on Russia?

Peter's impact upon Russia was unquestionably profound. Yet we might question whether it was as profound as he intended. We might argue that there were fundamental weaknesses in the modernisation as undertaken by Peter. There was certainly a great surge in economic activity, but not of enterprise. There were steps taken to conform to western ideals of polite society. Nevertheless Peter, we might contend, could undermine them through his own controversial conduct. Nor was he perhaps as innovative in his westernisation as he might appear. There were others before Peter with a strong interest in the west. Vasily Golitsyn, Sophia's supporter and lover (see page 19), had a very western outlook. Nor was Peter the first Russian to copy the western custom of shaving. The Russian elite at least may have been readier for Peter's demands than appears at first sight. Furthermore there was nothing new in Russian rulers demanding lifelong service from their nobles, nor was serfdom a novelty. But Peter made far more excessive demands than had ever been made before. Demands which were resented. We must now turn to the question of how much support, and how much resistance, Peter encountered.

References

1 Lindsey Hughes, *Russia in the Age of Peter the Great* (Yale University Press, 1998), p. 195.
2 Peter Henry Bruce, *Memoirs of Peter Henry Bruce, Esq., A Military Officer in the Services of Prussia, Russia and Great Britain* (Frank Cass, 1970), pp. 180–81.
3 John Perry, *The State of Russia under the Present Czar* (Frank Cass, 1967), pp. 268–69.
4 M.S. Anderson, *Peter the Great* (Thames & Hudson, 1978), p. 105.
5 Table of Ranks, 24 January 1722, Basil Dmytryshyn (ed.), *Imperial Russia: a Source Book, 1700–1917* (The Dryden Press, 1974), p. 17.

Working on chapter 6

Summary Diagram
Transforming Russian society

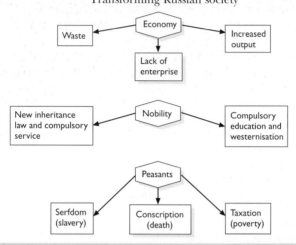

Structured and essay questions on Chapter 6

These make an occasional appearance in examinations, and are worth taking the time to consider.

I. a) Why did Peter rely so heavily on coercion in his attempts to transform Russia?

   b) How far did his over-reliance on the role of the state account for Peter's limited success in Westernising Russia?

2. To what extent have the achievements of Peter the Great in his economic and social policies been exaggerated?

In answering the first section of question 1, obviously yet again brevity and relevance are crucial. The second section again calls for analysis. As well as over-reliance on the state, which of course you must explain, what other factors hampered Peter's policies? You might want to consider historical disincentives to enterprise, the vast size of Russia, problems with importing expertise. Are there any other factors you might raise?

Question 2 invites you to assess the impact of these reforms. Where were the successes, and where can you find failures? It is up to you to analyse which were the most significant, and if, indeed, there was a significant gap between aims and achievements. Remember that his main aim was military power, and he achieved this. Against this, however, must be set the huge cost and massive waste of his failures and his partial successes. In short, was military might worth the price Russia paid for it?

7 Collaborators and Resistors

POINTS TO CONSIDER

What support did Peter have, and where did he find it? Also, what forms of resistance did he encounter and how effective were they? This chapter will introduce you to this crucial aspect of Peter's reign. In your reading consider whether the hatred he aroused is consistent with his claim to greatness.

KEY DATES

1698 *Streltsy* mutiny.
1705 Astrakhan revolt.
1707 Don Cossack revolt.
1708 Bashkir uprising, defection of Mazeppa.
1716 Alexis flees Russia.
1718 Death of Alexis.
1722 Law on imperial succession.

How much support did Peter have for his reforms? That there was considerable opposition is clear. Peter made unprecedented demands of his people, noble and peasant alike. He forced a deeply conservative and xenophobic nation to embrace western ways. Lifetime service was required, whether for the army officer or the serf. Peter, who saw himself as serving for life in his position, blithely assumed that if he must bear such a burden, everybody else should be content to do so. His taxes placed a crushing burden on the Russians. In addition, he mocked Russian traditions and seemed to vilify Russia's faith. Peter was, in short, bitterly hated. Yet can we accept that such hatred was universal? Surely if he had no supporters he could have achieved nothing?

1 Collaborators

> **KEY ISSUE** Who supported Peter and why?

Of course Peter did have supporters. Some shared, at least to some degree, his vision of a Russia which could face the west on equal terms. Others supported him because he was the sovereign, and they could not imagine doing otherwise. Many were simply opportunists, looking for advancement or rich pickings. A strong source of support came from the old nobility, men like Boris Golytsin and Boris Sheremetev. Their tradition of service, their upbringing as leaders and social standing made them essential to Peter. Though often resentful of the demands made of them and the novelties they had to accept, enough of the old nobility served Peter to make his reforms possible. There were also the new men, those who rose from obscurity to the highest positions, because their loyalty and competence attracted Peter's attention. Men like Menshikov and Peter Shafirov gave Peter invaluable support. Peter came to rely very heavily on the services of the Guards regiments. Peter's requirement that young nobles enlist in the ranks of the Guards gave them an *esprit de corps*, a sense of group identity and pride. The Guards became in fact training grounds in service to the Petrine state. Many of his most devoted supporters came from their ranks. The Guards regiments were also the usual, but not exclusive, route for the new men to rise in Peter's service.

Among his closest associates, most were hard drinkers and affable company. Here, perhaps, we might find a weakness in the way he chose his most trusted confederates. He preferred kindred spirits, who shared his taste for boisterous amusements and irreverent celebrations. The people he relied on most tended to be completely loyal, but few were honest. Among Peter's entourage those with a reputation for incorruptibility, men like Andrei Osterman, were rare exceptions. Fedor Romodanovsky, the Prince Caesar of his Drunken Synod, whom Peter treated with elaborate respect, was never accused of embezzlement. But the fact that he was the head of the *Preobrazhensky prikaz*, which Peter established as Russia's first regular secret police, might easily have deterred accusers. Most of Peter's closest circle were, however, utterly corrupt, assuming that lining their own pockets was a natural reward for their service. Peter's closest companion, Menshikov, was so frequently forgiven for embezzlement that it has been rumoured that their relationship was, at least in part, homosexual. Though this is mere speculation, the fact that the most corrupt could escape punishment did little to encourage honesty in others. In an attempt to battle corruption, in 1711 Peter established an office of informers, the *fiskaly*, the most notoriously and most hated being Alexis Nesterov, whose reports sent Matvei Gagarin, the governor of Siberia, to the gallows for corruption. Perhaps the scale of Peter's problem becomes clear when we learn that Nesterov was himself later executed for the same crime. Even his second wife and empress, Catherine, was implicated when it was found that members of her household were taking bribes, to encourage her to take up petitions and bring them to Peter's attention. They were not only corrupt, they tended to be quarrelsome, often feuding between themselves. Menshikov's arrogance and his jealousy of anyone appearing to challenge him for Peter's affections was a frequent source of such quarrels. Small wonder, perhaps, that Peter would discipline them with a heavy cudgel. Perhaps even more frustrating was the unwillingness of many of them, such as his Senate (see page 72), to take responsibility for fear of punishment for failure. When Peter's attention moved elsewhere, the projects he had started were always in danger of grinding to a halt.

-*Profile*-

Catherine I, empress of Russia (r. 1725–27). Born Martha Skavronskaya in 1684, she was a Lithuanian peasant from Sweden's Baltic empire. Orphaned at the age of three and raised as a servant by a Lutheran pastor, she was throughout her life illiterate. When Sheremetev captured the Livonian fortress town of Marienburg in 1702 she was one of the prisoners taken, and he took her into his own household before passing her on to Menshikov, who in turn passed her to Peter. She became his mistress, and in 1703 accepted the Orthodox faith and was re-Christened Catherine. A cheerful, sympathetic and hard-drinking companion, she was tough enough to accompany Peter on campaign. He found her support invaluable, and they were married in 1712.

She was crowned as empress consort in 1724. Upon Peter's death Menshikov bribed the Guards regiments to proclaim her empress. Her short reign was notable only for Menshikov's effective control of Russia.

Peter, it must be said, happily trampled on the sensibilities of his people, but he also actively sought willing support. He did so, for example, by prefacing his *ukazy* with explanations of why they were necessary and useful. Thus leather was ordered tanned with fish oil rather than the traditional birch bark because it would be more waterproof, and anyone who disobeyed was to be sent to the galleys for life. He was even willing to tolerate the Old Believers, provided that they were useful to the state, as were those who worked in the new mines at Olonets. But the Old Believers were essentially archconservatives, and few sects supported Peter. His toleration was strictly limited, and he eventually imposed heavier taxes and distinctive clothing on them. Despite Peter, their numbers seem to have increased, as conservatives offended by Peter's acts swelled their ranks.

2 The Nobles

> **KEY ISSUE** How could the nobles resist Peter's reforms?

Most of the nobility, even if they did not support Peter's reforms, conformed to his demands, at least while they were in his sight. But, like other Russian rulers, Peter had to contend with the sheer size of Russia. This itself could cause major problems. Too many officials and nobles far away from the centre of power could ignore Peter's commands with relative safety. They would disregard his *ukazy*, confident that they were far distant and he had not the resources to bring them to heel. In fact, if officials or nobles in a distant area were determined not to co-operate with Peter, they had a good chance of succeeding. He could only make examples of individuals. This was part of the massive inertia in Russia which Peter found so frustrating, despite all his efforts to make everyone perform useful service. Even near his capital his writ was not as powerful as he wished. Between 1718 and 1723 he issued 14 *ukazy* forbidding the use of old-fashioned, unseaworthy ships on lake Ladoga. They were all ignored. Even in Moscow, when Peter was absent, traditional dress reappeared. In Siberia his decrees on clothing and shaving made hardly any impact. His nobles made endless excuses to avoid service. Most, to reiterate, did serve willingly or grudgingly, but the opportunities for evasion still existed. This, we might conclude, was far more effective resistance than the open defiance which could be answered with force. Furthermore, if the nobles, few in number and readily identified, had a reasonable chance of evading Peter's demands, how effective was he in enforcing his will over the far more numerous and anonymous peasantry?

3 The Peasantry

> **KEY ISSUE** How could the peasants resist Peter?

Peter, as we have seen, was widely hated for the burdens he placed on the peasantry. Many of them found especially offensive his contempt for the Russia they held to be the only true Christian nation. The peasantry were bewildered by a tsar who did not behave as an Orthodox tsar and seemed bent on subverting Russia's traditions and faith. He could not, they decided, be the true tsar. The true tsar, after all, was a distant, pious and majestic figure. He certainly did not engage in drunken revelries with foreigners and defy Russian traditions. Rumours began to circulate that he was a changeling, the son of a foreigner, who had been substituted for Alexei's real son at birth. Alternatively, it was suggested that the real Peter had been kidnapped during the Great Embassy and substituted with a foreigner bent on destroying the Russians and damning their souls to hell. More alarming was the growing conviction that Peter was in reality the Antichrist, whose reign heralded the end of the world. This would make obedience to his demands positively sinful. So widespread were such stories that no brutality by the *Preobrazhensky prikaz* could silence them.

The penalties for defiance were savage. But the peasantry had a traditional form of resistance far more damaging, and harder for the state to combat – flight. Once a group of peasants reached the frontier area of the Cossacks, or Poland or the wilds of Siberia, they were free of taxes and service. Between 1719 and 1727 perhaps 200,000 fled. This was no minor matter: it was a mass migration of a significant part of the tax-paying population. Peter blamed the nobles for causing this flight by oppressing their serfs through their greed. However, his demands were the main cause, not least conscription. In 1718 alone 45,000 peasants avoided conscription and 20,000 deserted. Peter's reign saw a massive increase in brigandage and crime in general. Of course, most of the peasantry stayed and suffered their burdens. Further, not all flight led out of the country, some moved for greater economic opportunities within Russia. But even those who stayed were not necessarily co-operative.

The census of 1718 was obviously made in preparation for a new tax. Unsurprisingly peasants went to great lengths to avoid being counted. Aided by landowners anxious to avoid further tax burdens, there was massive concealment. In some districts perhaps half of the population was not counted. The census was not completed until 1722, and even then it proved to be so inaccurate that the army had to repeat it. There were still inaccuracies, but it was nevertheless used to assess the poll tax. A poll tax, because it ignores ability to pay, is inherently injust. But the offence it caused in Russia was far deeper. The poll tax, or *podushnaya podat*, literally translated as 'soul tax'. This was a shocking, indeed blasphemous, insult. The tsar, who had spent his reign in finding ever more necessities to tax, was now taxing their immortal souls! Small wonder that he was utterly detested and distrusted.

Even apparently sensible changes could be rejected. In a *ukaz* of 1721, Peter ordered all peasants to use scythes instead of sickles. This was backed up by an elaborate programme to train them in their use. It was a wasted effort. The peasants clung stubbornly to their sickles. They probably suspected that accepting the scythe would be followed by a new tax. In fact many of Peter's decrees were never enforced.

Despite all of the hostility Peter faced, however, we should not assume that it was universal. Though they had paid heavily for them, many peasants did welcome Peter's victories. They also approved of his 'inspiring hard labor [sic] . . . and his punishment of slackers, and also how he met the peasants'.[1] But that, of course, did not mean that they were content with the burdens he placed upon them, or that they would accept the novelties that he wanted to force on them. As a body the peasantry were hostile to Peter, but they were more likely to express their hostility through flight than rebellion. This did weaken the state, but it was not a positive menace to Peter.

4 Conspiracy

KEY ISSUE How serious were the conspiracies against Peter?

Aware he faced opposition, Peter established the *Preobrazhensky prikaz*, Russia's first permanent secret police. This was a brutal and effective body, charged with rooting out treason. Anyone aware of treason, by 'word or deed', was charged with reporting it on pain of death. Its head, Romodanovsky, never hesitated to use torture on even the most trivial cases. Yet, given the extent to which Peter was detested, the *Preobrazhensky prikaz* found astonishingly little evidence of any conspiracy against him. This is even more surprising as Peter took no precautions for his personal safety, regularly walking in St Petersburg unattended.

The nearest thing to a conspiracy came to light in March 1697, just before Peter departed on the Great Embassy. Two *boyars* and a *streltsy* officer were accused of plotting to assassinate the tsar. For this they were brutally executed. The evidence against them was flimsy, and it is entirely possible that there was no real conspiracy. The supposed conspirators had personal grievances, and might simply have complained too loudly about Peter's lifestyle. Grumbles about his friendship with foreigners, his disrespect for Russian traditions, how he had abandoned his wife, Moscow and now Russia, were to be standard complaints made about Peter. Perhaps Peter simply wanted to impress upon Russia the grim consequences of treason before he departed on an extensive tour abroad. The work of the *Preobrazhensky prikaz* was, by and large, limited to interrogating those who made unwise complaints. Grumbles by wives, blaming the tsar for absent husbands, by peasants against taxes, or by the traditionalists about Peter's irreligious lifestyle, were frequent. But they indicated widespread discontent, not conspiracy.

5 Revolts

KEY ISSUE Were the revolts against Peter serious?

a) The *Streltsy*

There was, of course, one group against whom Peter harboured the darkest suspicions and a deep grudge – the *streltsy*. The terrifying experience when they stormed the Kremlin and murdered his kinsmen had made a deep impression (see page 19). The *streltsy* had long been losing their elite status as they became an increasingly outdated force. Under Peter their standing diminished rapidly. Not unwisely when dealing with an untrustworthy force, Peter kept them as far from Moscow as possible, giving them onerous and dangerous duties in unpopular places such as Azov. Their casualties were high, they were separated from their families, and their businesses in Moscow suffered through their absence. Unsurprisingly morale suffered. Trouble broke out when Peter was absent in the west. In June 1698, four regiments of *streltsy*, ordered to march from Azov to the Polish frontier, mutinied and marched on Moscow. Reviving memories of the savagery of the last *streltsy* revolt caused some panic in the city. The revolt was in fact easily crushed by loyal troops supported by cannon. As many as 130 ringleaders were executed on the spot and nearly 1,900 prisoners taken.

This was not enough for Peter, who suspected a conspiracy and wanted to know what was planned and who was involved, especially if it was his deposed half-sister, Sophia. Nearly all the prisoners were tortured. Their resentments soon became clear: their casualties, absence from Moscow and loss of status, together with hostility towards foreigners. Like the peasantry, the *streltsy* were bewildered by a tsar who seemed bent on destroying Russia's traditions and faith, and concluded that he could not be the true tsar. There was no conspiracy, but this did not incline Peter to mercy. About 500 of the *streltsy* were branded and exiled, the rest perished in a series of mass executions. However the discontents they expressed still remained.

b) Revolts during the Great Northern War

There were, in fact, frequent localised risings throughout Russia during Peter's reign. But these were generally insignificant. There were, however, three serious revolts, which were all the more alarming as they broke out when the issue of the Great Northern War was still undecided. (See the map on page 105.)

In Astrakhan, another distant place of exile for the *streltsy*, trouble arose in 1705. Their now long-standing grievances against Peter seem to have been brought to a head by newly increased taxes and labour demands, and by a rumour that Peter had forbidden Russian men to marry for seven years, as he intended to give their women to foreigners. If the revolt had spread to the Don Cossacks – fiercely independent frontiersmen – the whole of the south east would have been in flames, which would have been really dangerous for Peter. He was sufficiently alarmed to offer leniency if the rebels submitted. But his promise of amnesty was taken as a sign of weakness. When Russian troops arrived to accept the city's surrender they met defiance. But fortunately for Peter the Cossacks did not support the rebels and they were quickly defeated by regular troops. Once again hundreds were tortured and executed. That the rebels believed the rumours of Peter banning marriages, and indeed claimed that his officials worshipped idols (which turned out to be the blocks upon which they stored their wigs), does show the depth to which he had become distrusted. There was little of which traditionalists did not believe him capable.

A further revolt broke out in 1708 among the Bashkirs, a nomadic Moslem people. They resented growing Russian colonisation of their lands and the taxation the Russians brought with them. With Charles XII actually marching on Russia this was acutely worrying. Peter was forced to detach three regiments from his armies facing the Swedes and called upon Buddhist Kalmyks – savage nomads who served in Russia's irregular cavalry – to deal with the rebels. The Kalmyks crushed the revolt and devastated the area.

Far more serious was the 1707 revolt of the Don Cossacks. They were antagonised by ever increasing Russian encroachment upon their lands and liberties. When Peter demanded that the Cossacks return army deserters and runaway serfs, he caused deep offence, as these were a traditional source of recruits. Most Cossack leaders were unwilling to defy Peter openly when he sent troops to enforce his demands. They preferred, instead, to go through the motions of co-operating while offering no real assistance. But one, Kondraty Bulavin, led a force to massacre the Russians. Loyal Cossacks defeated Bulavin, but he soon gathered a new force. By 1708 he was in a position to threaten Azov and Tagenrog. Alarmingly peasants, and even deserters from Peter's army, joined in the widespread but undirected violence. Peter had to send 10,000 troops, with Charles camped at Minsk. Bulavin aided in his own defeat by dividing his forces, which were defeated piecemeal.

Disunity and a lack of competent leaders were common to these revolts. Widespread and violent, and – with the war against Sweden in the balance – extremely worrying, they were still no real threat to Peter's throne. Further problems with the Cossacks were crushed with ease. Those tempted to support Mazeppa, the Cossack *hetman*, who deserted to the Swedes when Charles XII invaded Russia, were dealt with brutally (see page 51). Henceforth most Ukrainian Cossacks decided that loyalty to Peter was the wisest choice. Despite the enormous hostility he aroused, whenever Peter's authority was challenged he reacted quickly and ruthlessly. Did this explain why he never faced a revolt on the same massive scale as his father had faced from Stenka Razin (1670–71) or Catherine II would face from Emelian Pugachev (1773–75)? Perhaps he was lucky, and the rebels incompetent in that they put forward no pretender to the throne to

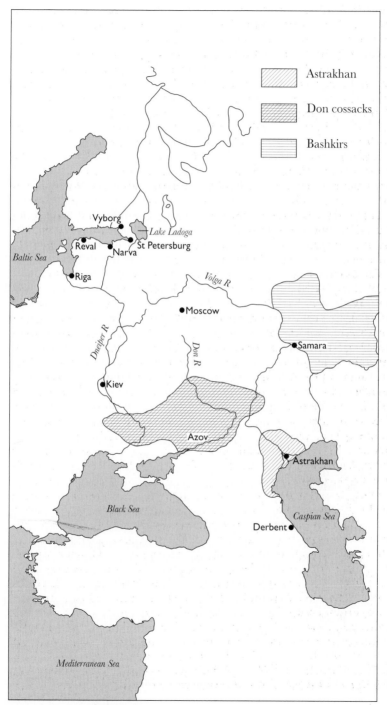

Rebellions against Peter the Great.

rally the disaffected. Given Russia's tradition of pretenders, and the fact that Peter was, in the minds of many, no true tsar, this is a surprising omission.

6 Alexis

> **KEY ISSUE** Why was Alexis a threat to Peter?

In common with other overbearing fathers, whose massive workload led them frequently to ignore their children, Peter was deeply disappointed in his heir. He was unable to comprehend that his son did not share his drive and passions. Alexis was, in fact, in many ways the antithesis of Peter. He lacked his father's unlimited energy and curiosity, having, for example, no taste for serving in the ranks. Rather than having a driving ambition to build a new Russia, Alexis was an admirer of Russia's traditional ways. One of the few things he shared with his father was his taste for heavy drinking. We should not be surprised to learn that he feared and detested his father. Also, we should be equally unsurprised to learn that all those who resented Peter's policies came to see in him their best hope. There was no conspiracy, but a deep, widely-felt longing for Peter to die and allow Alexis to restore the old ways to Russia. In consequence, Peter could not avoid coming to see Alexis as a threat to everything he wanted to achieve.

In October 1715 Peter resolved to settle the matter. He wrote his famous declaration to Alexis, threatening to remove him from the succession unless he made himself a worthy heir. It was a bitter tirade:

1 You have no inclination to learn the [art of] war, you do not apply yourself to it, and consequently you will never learn it: And how then can you command others, and judge of the reward which those deserve who do their duty, or punish others who fail of it? ... You say that the
5 weak state of your health will not permit you to undergo the fatigues of war: This is an excuse which is no better than the rest. I desire no fatigues, but only an inclination. ... Remember your obstinacy and ill-nature, how often I reproached you with it, and even chastised you for it. ... You do not make the least endeavours, and all your pleasure
10 seems to consist in staying idle and lazy at home: Things of which you ought to be ashamed ... seem to make up your dearest delight, nor do you foresee the dangerous consequences of it for yourself and for the whole state. ... After considering all those great inconveniences ... [I have resolved] to see if you will mend. If not, I will have you know that
15 I will deprive you of the succession, as one may cut off a useless member.[2]

Nor was Peter alone in this assessment of Alexis. Weber, the Hanoverian ambassador, wrote that he had:

1   by continually frequenting vicious company contracted such corrupt
habits, as could not fail producing an aversion of him in all honest minds;
and not withstanding all representations, he was so far sunk in sensual-
ity that ... the Czar being at length by his son's perverse conduct
5 wrought into an abhorrence of his person, began to drop broad inti-
mations, that, unless he gave timely hopes of amendment, he might be
sure of ... being thrust into a convent, it being better to sever a useless
member from the body, than to suffer the corruption spread through
the whole.[3]

But instead of capitulating to Peter and promising to reform, Alexis
offered to renounce the succession.

Peter certainly had not wanted this answer. He was aware that such
a renunciation would mean little after his death. As the undoubted
legitimate heir, Alexis would still be able to claim the throne and have
a very good chance of winning it. Then Peter's reforms might all be
reversed. Alexis, when pressed further, claimed he was willing to
become a monk. But Peter was still frustrated, as even that was not an
irreversible step. Was this defiance disguised as submission? But
Alexis made the disastrous mistake of defying Peter openly. In
November 1716 he was ordered to meet Peter in Copenhagen for a
confrontation. Instead he fled secretly to Vienna. Charles VI, his relative through marriage, offered him sanctuary. Not until the following
September was he traced to Naples, where Peter's representatives
browbeat him into returning. He was promised that he would be forgiven, be allowed to marry his mistress and retire to a country estate.

Indeed in February 1718, in the Kremlin, Alexis was formally
pardoned and disinherited after confessing his faults and asking for
forgiveness. But there was a condition. Alexis was to name his accomplices. Peter, convinced that there must have been a conspiracy, was
determined to root out the guilty. Many of Alexis's servants, friends
and associates were arrested and tortured. As his investigation
widened he was stunned to discover that his first wife, Eudoxia, while
still confined to a convent, was living not as a nun but in the estate
due to Peter's wife, which she still thought herself. She had even
taken the commander of her guards, Stefan Glebov, as her lover.
Peter's investigations resulted in an extensive purge, with some,
including the Bishop of Rostov, being broken on the wheel. The
unfortunate Glebov was impaled. But there was no evidence of a conspiracy, just of widespread resentment and hopes that Alexis, once on
the throne, would abandon his father's innovations and return to the
old ways. This was Peter's dilemma. Alexis was barred from the throne
while Peter lived. But what would happen when Peter died? Would all
his works be destroyed? There was only one way to guarantee this
would not happen. Alexis was brought to trial on the grounds that he
had invalidated his pardon by failing to name all of his accomplices.
After confessing treason under torture he was condemned to death.

He was not executed but died in prison, probably as a result of his torture. Peter claimed he died of apoplexy, but few believed him. He was widely suspected of murdering his son.

This, of course, left the question of the succession open. But Peter had an answer of sorts. Henceforth, he declared, the sovereign would nominate his successor. As events transpired, he was unable to do so on his deathbed. Menshikov was quick to bribe the Guards into supporting the claim of Catherine. The crown had, in fact, been made elective, with the Guards enjoying the power once held by the *streltsy*. As a result, over the next four decades a bizarre, even grotesque, procession of characters occupied the Russian throne. They included, in Catherine I (1725–27) an illiterate Lithuanian peasant; in Anna (r. 1730–40) and Elizabeth (r. 1741–62), two women notorious for their sexual appetites; in Peter II (r. 1727–30) a teenage boy; in Ivan VI (r. 1740–41) a babe in arms; and in Peter III (r. 1762) a German drunkard. Stability only returned to the throne after the reign of Catherine II (r. 1762–96) – who was not only not a Romanov but not even a Russian, and she gained the throne through her husband's murder.

7 Conclusion

> **KEY ISSUE** Could Peter have avoided this opposition?

Throughout his reign Peter enjoyed the support of a close group of enthusiastic supporters, who gave him loyal service even if they were rarely honest. He also faced a vast pool of hostility and resistance. While this resistance could at times be violent and widespread, his throne was never seriously at risk. Open defiance, whether from Cossacks or from his son, was dealt with brutally. Still his plans were frustrated by the stubborn unwillingness of his people to co-operate, or through simple flight. Would it, in fact, have been possible for Peter to have undertaken his reforms without arousing the hostility that he did? Given the intense conservatism of his people, and his own disregard for their sensibilities and ruthless determination to make them change, probably not. Only by relenting in his great drive to change Russia could he have avoided the hostility he aroused – and would this not have meant that he would have ceased to be Peter the Great?

References

1 Nicholas V. Riasanovsky, *The Image of Peter the Great in Russian History and Thought* (Oxford University Press, 1985), p. 83.
2 Peter's declaration to Alexis, 11 October 1715, Basil Dmytryshyn (ed.),

Imperial Russia: a Source Book, 1700-1917 (The Dryden Press, 1974), pp. 22–24.

3 Friedrich Christian Weber, *The Present State of Russia* (Frank Cass & Co. Ltd., 1968), p. 105.

Working on chapter 7

Summary Diagram
Responses to Peter

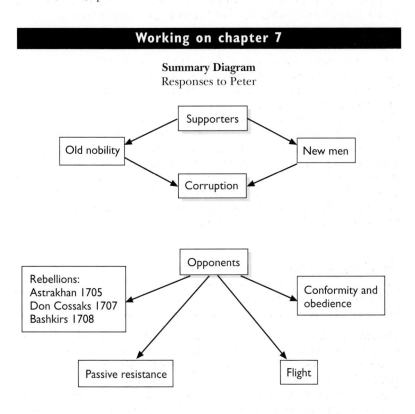

Source-based questions on Chapter 7

Read the extracts by Peter and Weber on pages 106 and 107 and answer the following questions.

a) What precisely was Peter's complaint against Alexis? (*6 marks*)
b) What did Weber mean by 'vicious company' and 'corrupt habits' (lines 1–2)? (*6 marks*)
c) Do these two accounts provide independent verification of Alexis's character? (*8 marks*)

Structured and essay questions on chapter 7

1. **a)** Why were Russians so hostile to Peter's reforms?
   b) How seriously was Peter challenged by the revolts he faced?
2. How serious was the opposition to the reforms of Peter the Great?